CW01506903

Marine life
of St Helena

by Judith Brown

with support from

Published by

First published 2014 by Pisces Publications for Saint Helena Government.
Pisces Publications is the imprint of NatureBureau.

British Library-in-Publication Data
A catalogue record for this book is available from the British Library.

ISBN 978 1 874357 64 3

Designed by NatureBureau, 36 Kingfisher Court, Hambridge Road, Newbury, Berkshire RG14 5SJ
www.naturebureau.co.uk

Companion books published by Pisces Publications

Mosses & Liverworts of St Helena ISBN 978 1 874357 51 3
Flowering Plants & Ferns of St Helena ISBN 978 1 874357 52 0
Lichens of St Helena ISBN 978 1 874357 53 7

Cover photographs
FRONT Blackbar soldierfish *Myripristis jacobus* and a St Helena wrasse *Thalassoma sanctaehelenae* (Steve Brown); green and black nudibranch *Tambja* sp. (Judith Brown), St Helena sea star *Astropecten sanctaehelenae* (Judith Brown), St Helena sharpenose pufferfish *Canthigaster sanctaehelenae* (Steve Brown)
BACK Orange cup coral *Balanophyllia helenae* (Judith Brown)

Contents

Acknowledgements --- iv

Introduction --- 1

PORIFERA --- 2

CNIDARIA --- 15

PLATYHELMINTHES --- 33

ANNELIDA --- 37

ARTHROPODA -- 43

BRYOZOA -- 65

MOLLUSCA -- 69

ECHINODERMATA --- 97

CHORDATA

    Ascidiacea --- 109

    Chondrichthyes -- 115

    Actinopterygii -- 119

    Reptilia --- 175

    Mammalia --- 179

    Aves --- 185

ALGAE -- 195

WRECKS -- 203

Glossary --- 213

References -- 214

Index --- 216

Acknowledgements

The publication of this book and the marine research including diving survey work were part of a Darwin Initiative funded marine biodiversity project (Project 19-031) which was in joint partnership with the Joint Nature Conservation Committee (JNCC) and the Environmental Management Division (EMD) of St Helena Government.

This work is a combined effort in particular from all staff members of the marine section of EMD, their hard work and friendship made my two years on St Helena very special – thankyou Elizabeth Clingham, Leeann Henry and Annalea Beard. Special thanks and recognition go to Steve Brown for all his efforts with the underwater cameras, filling dive cylinders and making/mending equipment and who is responsible for a large percentage of the beautiful marine images.

This book would not have been possible without the help of the following taxonomists who have generously given their expertise in identifying St Helena's marine species: Drs Michael Schröedl & Vinicius Padula, University of Munich (for Opisthobranchs); Juliana Bahia, University of Munich (for flatworms); Dr Sammy de Grave, Oxford Museum of Natural History (for shrimps); Dr Paul Clark, Natural History Museum (for crabs); Dr Felix Lorenz, Germany (for Ovulids and Conus); Dr Ronald Fricke (for fish); Mr Frank Swinnen, Belgium (for molluscs); Dr James Reimer, University of the Ryukyus (for Zoanthids); Dr Alfonso Ramos, Universidad de Alicante (for ascidians); Ms Beatriz Riverea, Universidad Nacional Autónoma de México (for fireworms); Dr Claire Goodwin, Natural History Museum of Northern Ireland (for sponges); Dr Björn Berning, Upper Austrian State Museum (for Bryozoans); Helmut Zibrowius, France (for corals); Dr Horia Galea, Hydrozoan Research Laboratory, France (for Hydroids); Prof Dave Meyer, University of Carolina (for Crinoids); Dr Eijiroh Nishi, Japan (for the devil worm); Dr Pawson, Smithsonian Institution, Washington DC, USA (for Echinoderms); Michael Amor, La Trobe University, Australia (for octopus) and Dr Peter Wirtz (for everything, in particular his boundless knowledge and enthusiasm for all marine critters!).

This book has been transformed by the skill and dedication of the NatureBureau team – Peter Creed for his creative layouts and patience with my many corrections and Aurea Paquete for sorting the many images and her fantastic cover.

For their diving support and many happy memories both above and below water Craig Yon, Keith Yon, Graham Sim, Anthony Thomas, Johnny Herne and Jeremy Clingham. And to my many other dive buddies who put up with me paying more attention to a sea slug than to them. Thanks also to Robert Bedwell and the crew of the Gannett III.

All photographs are taken by the marine section staff and the divers mentioned above apart from cetaceans (David Higgins), breaching humpback whale (Richard Moors), tuna and dolphinfish (Terry Brennan), Portuguese man-of-war (Joe Hollins), red-footed booby (Phil Lambdon), all other seabirds (David Jenkins) and the dive site map (Sam Cherrett). Argos Atlantic Coldstore also kindly called whenever any unusual fish were brought in.

Introduction

St Helena is an isolated island surrounded by the rich waters of the South Atlantic and its marine environment supports a diverse array of marine life, including many endemics. The surrounding ocean is also important for several charismatic migratory species including humpback whales, whale sharks and turtles as well as resident populations of dolphins. As an island situated in the middle of the South Atlantic, St Helena is dependent in many ways on the waters surrounding it, particularly providing an access route bringing in supplies and people. The marine environment

supports a range of both recreational and commercial activities, from dolphin and whale watching trips to inshore pole and line fishing.

St Helena is an old (over 14 million years) volcanic island rising to 820m above sea-level at its highest point. It has an area of 120km² (17km by 10km) and is 930km east of the mid-Atlantic ridge. The island has a shelf area of 185km² and the 200 mile territorial sea comprises of 444,916km². Within the territorial sea lie two major seamounts which rise to less than 100m water depth. The Cardno seamount (12° 54.00′ S, 6° 03.00′ W) is approximately 180nm to the north of St Helena and Bonaparte seamount (15° 38.40′ S, 6° 58.20′ W) is around 80nm to the west of St Helena. Two deeper seamounts also exist within the territorial waters, Sysoev seamount lies to the east and close to Bonaparte and Akademic Kurchakov seamount lies further to the west of Bonaparte. The seamounts which lie within the St Helena economic zone comprise 0.2% of the world's seamounts.

St Helena butterflyfish *Chaetodon sanctaehelenae* and diver at Long Ledge, one of the most popular dive sites

Due to the steep nature of the St Helena's cliffs as they enter the sea there is limited littoral habitat, with only three beach areas with easy access (Sandy Bay [considered unsafe for swimmers], Rupert's Bay and James Bay). The tidal range is also small ranging from 0.5m during neap tides to 1.25m during spring tides. Large rock pools are present at Lot's Wife's Ponds, with much smaller pools at Lemon Valley, Sandy Bay, Banks, Rupert's, Birdown, Sharks Valley, and some other much less accessible areas.

The Benguela current flows northward from Cape Point, South Africa driven by the Southeast Trade Winds. The winds also drive the South Atlantic Gyre which in turn carries these cool waters towards St Helena, resulting in sea surface temperatures of between 19°C (winter) and 25°C (summer). The movements of both the surface and subsurface currents over many years has resulted in a mixed marine fauna in the waters of St Helena including western Atlantic, eastern Atlantic and circumtropical species.

Nearly 780 marine species have so far been recorded from St Helena including 72 species of algae, 223 Mollusca, 44 Echinodermata, 173 Chordata (including 10 Ascidacea), 41 Cnidaria, 33 Bryozoa, 69 Formanifera, 64 Crustacea, 24 Porifera, 31 Annelida and 5 Plathelminthes. Of these at least 50 are endemic species and work continues to further describe species which have recently been discovered. This guide does not cover all the species found in St Helena's waters but instead details the common species found in the shallow waters as well as some of the commercial species found further offshore.

Inshore habitats include large boulder and bedrock reefs; both white and volcanic sandy areas and regions covered in cobbles and maerl. Although there are no reef-building corals around St Helena there are ten species of octocoral including the beautiful endemic orange cup coral which covers the underside of ledges and roofs of caves. Divers should take time to explore all the different habitats to see the full range of beautiful and unusual species St Helena has to offer. And don't forget to venture out when it gets dark to see the multitude of night creatures that remain hidden during daylight, including the endemic Melliss's conger.

Worldwide there are increasing pressures on the marine environment both through human intervention and through climate change. Globally habitats, species abundance and species diversity have been damaged through overexploitation or destructive methods of extracting the natural resources, through intentional or accidental pollution and through careless or misguided usage of the marine ecosystem. It is imperative to protect the relatively pristine environment which exists around St Helena for future generations to enjoy. St Helena is a UK Overseas territory, administered by the Government of St Helena, and the marine section of the government works alongside recreational marine uses and commercial businesses to protect the unique marine ecosystem and the exceptional biodiversity which it supports.

The green and black nudibranch *Tambja* sp. eating the bryozoan *Bugula* cf. *dentata* off Speery Island

PORIFERA

PORIFERA

The simplest of the multicellular animals are the sponges whose bodies comprise of numerous pores (hence the scientific name for the Phylum Porifera meaning pore bearer). Beating of flagella (tiny hairs) creates a current which draws water through the pores into the sponge. Food particles and oxygen are filtered from the water through net like cells and the water then leaves the sponge through larger pores called oscula. Their skeleton is comprised of the protein collagen and either calcareous or silica spicules. Reproduction can be both asexual, by fragmentation, or sexual, with each sponge being both male and female and sperm being released into the water column.

Globally there are around 5,000 species of sponge with at least 27 species found at St Helena with a range of different colours and forms and occupying different habitats. Sponges are sessile benthic species and can be either encrusting or free standing forming tubes, barrels, balls or mounds and ranging in size from less than a few centimetres to more than a metre. Some sponges produce toxins which ward off predators and also prevent species growing on them; however the chemicals they produce have also been beneficial in human medicine.

There are three distinct groups in the Phylum Porifera, the Hexactinellida (glass sponges – usually very deep water), the Demospongia, and the Calcarea (calcareous sponges).

Colourful sponges encrust rocky habitats, some species forming turrets

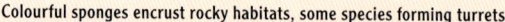

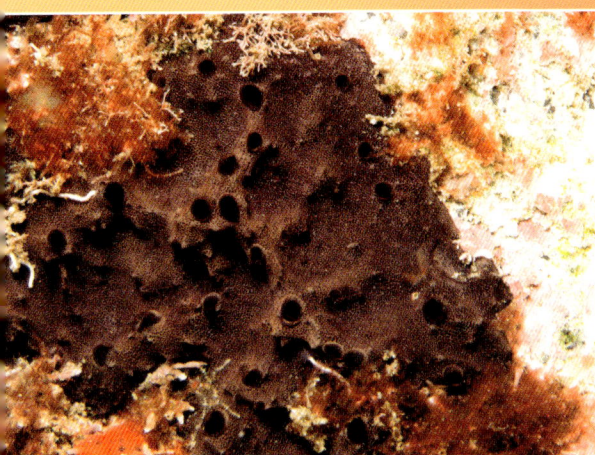

DEMOSPONGIA
(keratose demosponges)

Dictyoceratida (order)
Dark black/purple massively encrusting sponge with porous surface. Tough but compressible. Wiry sponging filaments protruding from tissue.

Euryspongia sp.
Beige to pale mustard crust with connulose surface. Some debris present on surface between connules. Compressible. Individual sponging fibres visible at edge. Many inclusions of sand etc.

Euryspongia sp.
Thickly encrusting pale yellow sponge, overgrowing bryozoan.

Aplysilla sp.

Massively encrusting coral-pink sponge with connulose surface. Connules joined by a distinct meshwork of fibres. A few large oscules. Texture soft and compressible. *Aplysilla* is defined as a Darwinellidae in which the sponge is always encrusting. Typically the fibres of the skeleton are unbranched but in some species branching may be frequent.

Aplysilla sp.

Lemon/cream encrusting sponge with many oscules/ostia visible on surface.

Sarcotragus sp.

Bright fluorescent yellow crust with connulose surface. Large, raised, oscules present at intervals. Wiry texture with obvious filaments but easy to pull apart. Produced a lot of slime when sampled for identification.

Dysidea sp.
Low pale grey crust with prominent large oscules. Connulose surface with web of fibres connecting connules.

Ircina sp.
Dark charcoal-coloured cushion-shaped sponge with large oscules. Elastic and compressible.

Chondrosia cf. *plebeja*
Very hard white lump >15mm thick. Dark lines visible in tissue.

Cacospongia sp.
The sponge is encrusting on a sponge crab *Dromia* sp. It is a low black crust (2–4mm). Tough texture, not easy to tear, with wiry filaments visible. Connulose surface.

Dysidea sp.
White sponge found on back of a sponge crab *Dromia* sp. Approximately 6mm thick, very compressible. Surface strongly connulose with a pronounced network of fibres between the connules.

Verongula sp.
Pale peach sponge with the surface covered in low rounded mounds. Each of these mounds bears a terminal oscule. Pattern formed by large fibres clearly visible on sponge surface and surface between in low folds giving a honeycomb like appearance.

Aplysina sp.
Bright yellow sponge. Silt encrusted base bearing several large mounds, each with a terminal oscule. Sponge surface covered in small mounds. Tough texture.

Aplysina sp.
Massive, dull orange, encrusting sponge with numerous lobes on its surface. Areas of pore sieves with many oscules and ostia irregularly dispersed over surface. Stalked lobe 20mm in height. Connulose surface.

DEMOSPONGIA
(demosponges with spicules)

Desmanthus sp.
Thin, bright orange (<1mm) crust.
Relatively common in caves and
under ledges

Hymeniacidon sp.
Bright orange, thickly encrusting
sponge (up to 4mm in height)
with some raised oscules. Surface
has a distinctive pattern of white
marks — presumably caused by
sand inclusions.

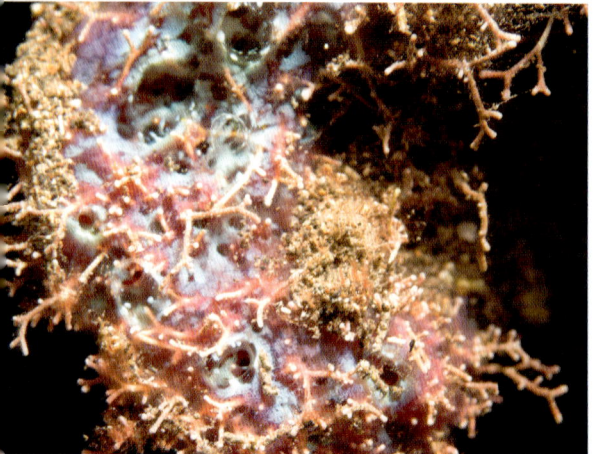

Stelleta sp.
Pale mauve encrusting sponge
growing over bryozoan. Produced
lots of slime when sampled for
identification.

Mycale (_Mycale_) sp.
Thickly encrusting, pale yellow sponge with small mounds on its surface. This is a new species to science and is currently being described.

Aaptos sp.
Yellow encrusting sponge approximately 2mm thick. Some large oscules. Very firm with a smooth, slimy feeling, surface.

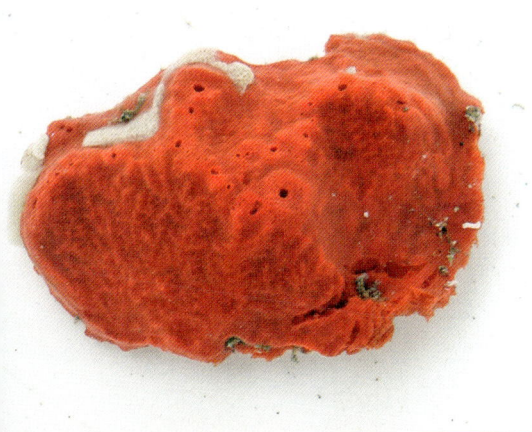

Tedania (_Tedania_) sp.
Massively encrusting red-orange sponge with velvety surface bearing a few small oscules approximately 5mm thick. Smooth surface. This is a new species to science and is currently being described.

Tedania (*Tedania*) sp.
Orange volcano sponge
Bright red-orange lobe sponge
bearing two large oscules
approximately 5mm thick. Smooth
surface bearing veins, which in
some areas are raised into ridges.
Some sand inclusions.

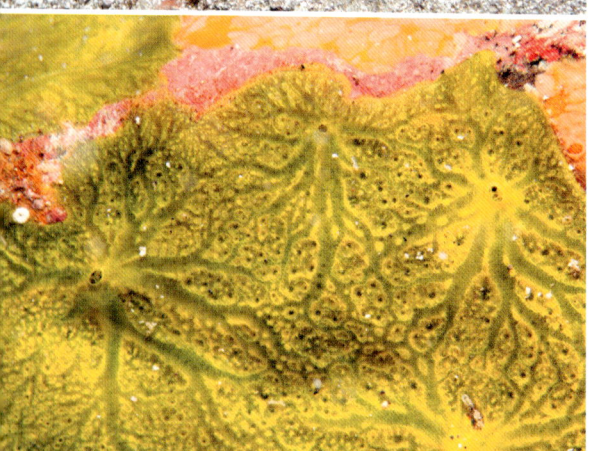

Hymedesmiidae (family)
Yellow crust with prominent,
dark green, star shaped veins
with connecting channel
giving a mottled appearance.
Approximately 2mm thick.
Breaks easily. Many inclusions of
sand etc.

CALCAREA

Grantia (?) sp.
Grey-white lobe 10mm thick.
Firm, very smooth, surface. A few
very large oscules.

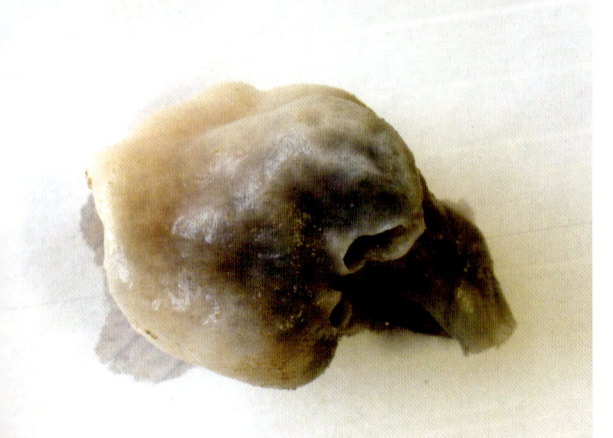

Ute (?) sp.

White folded sponge composed of a joined series of lobes. Many of these have terminal oscules. Up to 5mm thick. Very smooth surface with large oscules.

Ute sp.

Very long tubular white sponge (whole not shown in picture). Hispid (rough with stiff spines) surface. Opening down length fringed with protruding spicules. Several found around Lighter Rock in July. This is a new species to science and is currently being described.

Leucandra sp.
Hairy tube sponge
Short thin-walled globular sponge with large internal cavity (10mm length by 50mm diameter). Tuft of spicules around atrium.

Amphoriscidae (family)
Thin-walled vase-shaped sponge with shiny surface. Small (<10mm).

CNIDARIA

CNIDARIA

Cnidaria comes from the Greek meaning nettle and refers to the unique characteristic of this group in having stinging cells called nematocysts or cnidocytes. The nematocyst are used for catching prey or for protecting themselves from predators. Cnidaria have radial symmetry and can be solitary animals or can form colonies which can be very large. All have a central mouth with encircling tentacles and are either sedentary (a polyp) or are free swimming (medusa). In corals and hydroids the polyps are housed within a skeleton made from lime or chiton. Cnidarian are organised by a simple nervous system and feed either by predation, absorbing dissolved organic nutrients, filtering food particles out of the water, or by obtaining nutrients from symbiotic algae which live within its cells. Regeneration in cnidarians allows them to recover from injuries as well as reproduce asexually by budding or fragmentation. Sexual reproduction also occurs; often involving a complex lifecycle involving both medusa and polyp forms.

This Phylum contains over 10,000 species globally with over 37 found in St Helena including several endemics. There are four classes in the Phylum Cnidaria, the Anthozoa (including true corals, anemones, zoanthids and sea fans); the Cubozoa (the box jellies which often have highly potent toxins); the Scyphozoa (true jellyfish); and the Hydrozoa.

The spectacular black fan coral *Plumapathes pennacea* on a vertical wall

The endemic orange cup coral *Balanophyllia helenae* brightens up the rocky walls on which it lives

The common white encrusting zoanthid *Palythoa caribbaeorum* often covers large areas of boulders in shallow waters

ACTINARIA

Phymactis sanctaehelenae
Common sea anemone

This large species has a broad column densely covered in many vesicles and it has numerous tentacles (>300). The column colour is dark red brown to almost black with slightly brighter red-brown tentacles. Found along the rocky coast at the water line, including in James Bay. Endemic to St Helena.

Pseudactinia varia
False plum anemone

The column is smooth and coloured orange with pale yellow, purple-tipped, tentacles. Recorded in shallow depths 2–12m in James Bay, Munden's Point and Roman's reef attached to rocks. Found in South Africa and St Helena.

Telmatactis cricoides
Club-tipped anemone
Derives its name from the club-like tips to the end of each tentacle. A dirty orange-brown column with highly variable coloration of tentacles including orange, dirty orange to blue and white mottled with pale brown. Generally found under rocks and in dark crevices in depths of 5–40m. The anemone shrimp *Thor* cf. *manningi* is often associated with the anemone using the stinging tentacles for protection.

Two other species of *Telmatactis* are found in St Helena waters **Telmatactis forskalii Forskal's sea anemone** (bottom left) and **Telmatactis solidago** (bottom right).

Isarachnanthus maderensis
Banded tube anemone

A variety of colour morphs exist (pale to dark brown/white, pink/white, orange/white) each with distinctive banding on the tentacles. A nocturnal species they are completely withdrawn into rock crevices during the day. Found in depths of 5–20m and distributed throughout the north and central Atlantic.

Aiptasia insignis
Trumpet anemone

Tentacles are long and thin and are pale yellow-brown to transparent in colour with white banding. Generally found in tide pools (very common in Lot's Wife's Ponds) and shallow water on rocky substrate. Dense colonies are often found close together as reproduction is by budding – small sections of the basal plate detach and can grow into new anemones quickly. *Aiptasia* species often have algae cells living in their tentacles which provide food for the host through photosynthesis. Reaches a height up to 2cm with less than 96 tentacles. Endemic to St Helena.

Anthothoe affinis
Striped anemone
This species is usually found attached to the shell of the hermit crab *Dardanus imperator*, offering the crab a means of protection. Column is smooth and is yellow with dark grey banding with up to 200 white tentacles.

Antipathozoanthus sp.
Golden encrusting zoanthid
Bright golden to yellow-coloured tentacles and body. Found in dark places under ledges or in caves encrusting rock surfaces or encrusting the stems of the black fan coral *Plumapathes pennacea*.

Pachycerianthus sp.
Burrowing anemone

This tube-dwelling anemone is found buried in sediment in muddy and sandy substrates. The tube can be very long. Variable colour from translucent to peachy orange to pale brown. Numerous tentacles (>80) occur in two rows and it uses its stinging cells to catch its prey, most likely small crustaceans.

Palythoa caribbaeorum
White encrusting zoanthid

Very common in shallow water especially areas with some water movement. Occurs in dense mats often covering whole boulders. Each polyp has an oral disc with two rows of short tentacles. When disturbed the tentacles retract leaving small bumps. Off-white to yellow in colour.

Isaurus sp.
Lumpy finger zoanthid

Pale white to pale green in colour reaching a size of about 8cm. The small tentacles are extended only at night to feed, however they also contain algae which provides the zoanthid with nutrients from photosynthesis. The long cylindrical body has a gnarled warty appearance. Currently only recorded on rocky substrate at Sharks valley and Billy May's Revenge (in 8m).

Zoanthid sp.

Other species of zoanthid have been reported in St Helena waters including *Protopalythoa canariense* Canarian sea mat (left), *Palythoa* sp. Yellow zoanthid (below left – only a single record from Ruperts Bay) and several species still to be fully identified (example below right). They can be a variety of colours and are distinguished by their two rows of tentacles.

OCTOCORALIA

Balanophyllia helenae
Orange cup coral

A beautiful bright orange or yellow stony cup coral. The solitary polyps are usually found in large numbers on the roofs of caves, on vertical rocky faces and under overhangs. It uses its polyp tentacles to feed on plankton. Endemic to St Helena.

Polycyathus atlanticus

A small (<1cm) round stony coral with almost transparent tissue coming out of a calcareous "cup" or corallites which is white with a slight hint of colour from orange to pink to light brown. The cups protrude from a thin encrusting base, although this is often overgrown by sponge or algae making the corallites seem unconnected. Found in dark places under ledges and in caves.

Madracis sp.

Colonies are thinly encrusting over rocks, sometimes with raised lobes. The colony surface is densely covered with very small polyps making it appear fuzzy when the polyps are extended. Coloration is light brown, yellow, pink or olive green.

Favia gravida
Star coral

Distributed along the coast of Brazil, east Africa, Ascension and St Helena this coral forms small crusts on rocky habitats. Usually less than 7cm they are light yellow to greenish-brown in colour. Common in shallow water. It reproduces asexually by fragmentation and also by budding.

Sclerhelia hirtella
St Helena tree coral
A branched coral with variable colour from orange to brown to pink. Generally found in deeper water although recorded from 12m on the wreck of the Papa Nui. Found in isolated colonies usually less than 15cm tall. Endemic to St Helena

Gorgonia
Rose lace gorgonian
Found on the seabed in caves, or on dark vertical faces. Delicate and susceptible to damage from careless diver's fins

Carijoa rilsel
Snowflake coral
Erect branched dirty white stems which can often be overgrown with algae making them reddish-brown in colour, and bright white polyps each with eight tentacles. It has small stinging cells in its tentacles which it uses to capture zooplankton. Native to the western Atlantic, in other areas it is an introduced species most likely transported on the hulls of ships. It has only been recorded on St Helena at Speery Island.

Plumapathes pennacea
Black fan coral

Dull grey to brownish-grey in colour with many feather-like branches extending in various directions. It can be found under overhangs and in caves. Often wing oysters and occasionally ovulids are found living on the branches, which can also sometimes be covered in the golden encrusting zoanthid *Antipathzoanthus*. Recorded from the Indo-Pacific and southern and western Atlantic. They are a long-lived and slow-growing species.

Stichopathes filiformis
Wire coral

A long slender unbranched stalk with polyp tentacles coming out of one side only. Colour varies from white to pale brown to green. They reach a length of up to 200cm. Generally in water deeper than 20m they grow along vertical rock faces.

HYDROZOA

Macrorhynchia filamentosa
Smoky feather hydroid

A black to dark purple feather-shaped colonial animal living on stems of up to 15cm high. Distributed in the southern hemisphere in depths from 0–80m on rocky habitats. Relatively uncommon on St Helena it has been recorded at Bird Island, Speery Island and Southwest Point.

Macrorhynchia philippina
Golden sea fern

The nematocysts (stinging cells) of this hydroid make it one to avoid touching. This brown-stemmed hydroid has white feather-like branches. Common on rocky habitats.

Aglaophenia parvula

A central stalk with cream to white alternating branches. Found in tropical and temperate seas worldwide in depths to 15m. Prefers wave exposed areas.

Aglaophenia cf. *picardi*
Sea fern

Alternating branches on a fine olive green/brown to white-coloured stem. Prefer shaded or dark habitats with moderate to strong wave exposure. Found in depths of 3–10m though occasionally down to 30m.

Sertularia marginata
A small fern-shaped colonial hydroid. Alternating white branches (often with algal growth) coming off a main stem. Each branch with regularly spaced pairs of white/translucent polyps.

Sertularia turbinata
Unbranched hydroid
A single unbranched stem with regularly spaced pairs of white/translucent polyps which come off either side of the stem. Often the stem is covered in algae. A colonial species with fixed gonophores.

Pennaria disticha
Christmas tree hydroid
or sea nettle

Bright white single polyps on the tips of the branches which come off a thick black central stem. Common on rocky habitats but also grow on ropes, shipwrecks and out of sponges. Often found in groups in areas with current. It has stinging cells which it uses with its small tentacles to trap plankton. Grows up to 30cm and lives in depths down to 40m.

Eudendrium carneum
Red stick hydroid
An olive-brown stem with branches bearing translucent pink polyps, each sub-branch bearing several polyps. This colonial hydroid has a circum-subtropical distribution.

Eudendrium ramosum
A bush-like colony of central stalks with many angular primary and sub-branches each terminating in a white polyp. Stem often covered in algae or cyanobacteria.

Ectopleura cf. mayeri

This hydroid has a short stem (up to 2cm) and lives in small colonies. Stem with single polyp with up to 16 tentacles. Gonophores released as free medusae, medusae when released and when mature have only two tentacles. Found in depths of 0.5–40m.

Zyzzyzus sp.
Solitary sponge hydroid

A solitary polyp with translucent tentacles and stalk making it difficult to see. Attaches itself to sponges on rocky areas. Several individuals often found on same sponge. It will sting if touched.

Velella velella
Purple sail

[not illustrated]
Found at the ocean surface this free-floating hydrozoan colony uses a sail to transport itself across the sea surface. They catch their plankton prey by use of stinging tentacles which hang below the sail in the water. It is blue in coloration and can often be seen washed up at Sandy Bay beach.

Physalia physalis
Portuguese man-of-war

A colonial hydrozoan (not a jellyfish), *Physalia physalia* is transported around the oceans by winds and currents using a gas-filled bladder as a means of propulsion. It is a carnivorous species using its highly toxic stinging cells to paralyse small fish and plankton. Often found washed up on Sandy Bay beach in large numbers.

PLATYHELMINTHES

PLATYHELMINTHES

Marine flatworms are thin flat-bodied species that generally hide under rocks during the day, coming out at night to feed. They are predators on sessile invertebrates including ascidians, sponges and bryozoans (although some species do feed on green algae). They secrete a protein-dissolving compound and this digestive enzyme breaks down the invertebrates' body tissues which they then suck up through their mouth. Folds in the margin of their body form antennae on their head which are sensory organs and some have simple eye-spots used in the detection of light. They are often brightly coloured to deter predators however they can regenerate sections of their body if damaged. Although individuals are both male and female (simultaneous hermaphrodites) they partake in sexual reproduction, injecting sperm into the body of another flatworm which then moves within the body to the female reproductive organ. They breathe via diffusion through their body surface. In this chapter within the Phylum Platyhelminthes, we are just considering here the polyclads (animals of the order Polycladida).

Often hidden under rocks, flatworms can also be very well camouflaged, such as *Pericelis* cf. *cata* (left) and *Acotylea* sp. (below), making them hard to spot

Pseudoceros sp.
All black flatworm.

Enchiridium cf. _periommatum_
White body covered in tiny brown spots. Brown stripe centrally down length of body. Distributed in the Caribbean and St Helena.

Pericelis cf. *cata*
Mottled white and light brown body with darker brown spots. Distributed in Curaçao, Brazil and St Helena.

Acotylea sp.
Pale brown to almost translucent body with a slightly darker central longitudinal stripe.

Pseudobiceros cf. *pardalis*
Black to dark purple body with bright yellow and white spots. Distributed in Bermuda, Bahamas, Florida, Panama, Brazil and St Helena.

ANNELIDA

ANNELIDA

The distinguishing feature of the Annelids or ring worms is the segmented body. In the class Polychaeta each segment bears outgrowths called parapodia which it uses in locomotion. Polychaetes are commonly referred to as bristleworms so-called for the multiple chaetae or hairs. Polychaetes can be free-living or sedentary, living within tubes made from sand grains, fibres or within calcareous shells.

The sub phylum Echiura (spoon worms) are unsegmented worms with a soft sac-like body and an extendable probiscus. They are suspension feeders and breathe by absorbing oxygen through their body wall. Worldwide there are over 230 species of Echiura living in sand or mud burrows or in crevices in the rock.

The sub phylum Sipunculida (peanut worms) have a thick, tough skin on an unsegmented body with a retractable section referred to as the introvert. Short tentacles surround the mouth at the end of the introvert which they use to feed on organic detritus on the seabed.

The sedentary devil worm *Lygdamis wirtzi* (above) is common in St Helena, found on sandy and gravel areas

Feather duster worm *Bispira* sp. (left) are tiny polychaetes found in rocky habitats, often with their tubes encrusted with algae.

Hermodice carunculata
Bearded fireworm

This bristleworm is very common on rocky habitats. Its white hairs are venomous containing a neurotoxin which causes irritation to the skin if touched. Common size up to 10cm (though can reach 35cm) they flare their bristles if disturbed. Found in the tropical western Atlantic, Ascension and St Helena. Fireworms predate on cnidarians in particular hard and soft corals and anemones, though they will also feed on small crustaceans and can be seen in large numbers preying on dead animals on the seafloor. The females produce a phosphorescent glow when they are ready to mate which attracts the males.

Eurythoe complanata

A nocturnal species found hidden under rocks and boulders during the day, coming out at night to feed mainly on carrion but also on corals and algae. An Atlantic species which can reproduce both asexually by fragmentation and sexually as a broadcast spawner, releasing eggs and sperm into the water column. Body pink in coloration with venomous white bristles.

Hesione pantherina
Leopard worm

This carnivorous polychaete has numerous red spots on its white body and has white walking leg bristles. Found in depths greater than 5m on rocky habitats, hidden beneath stones during the day. Reaches a maximum length of 7cm.

Lygdamis wirtzi
Devil worm

This shallow water Sabellariidae is found on coarse sand and cobble substrates. It makes its tube from small fragments of shell and stones. The tube can reach lengths of up to 30cm, however most of its tube is often buried in the sand. It gets its name from the two devils' horns with which it feeds, filtering planktonic particles from the water. If threatened it withdraws its soft body into its tube, as the picture (below left) of a *Lygdamis* sp. shows.

Phascolosoma (Phascolosoma) stephensoni Peanut worm

This bilaterally symmetrical, unsegmented marine worm is light brown in colour with darker patches. They are infaunal animals, living burrowed in sediment or hidden within coral rubble or under stones. It has two sections – its main body and a long proboscis which it can retract. It feeds on organic matter or detritus trapped in the sand.

Ochetostoma baronii Green rock echiuran

The vivid green coloration of the echiurid is due to Bonellin, a chemical pigment in its skin which is highly toxic to other organisms. It has an extendable feeding proboscis on one end of its rotund body with which it brings detritus to its mouth.

Chaetopterus variopedatus
Parchment worm

This segmented marine bristleworm can reach up to 25cm long. It pumps water through the papery tube in which it lives, with food particles becoming trapped on a mucus bag. Females can produce up to 1 million eggs which are released into the water column to be fertilised. If damaged it can regenerate its whole body from a single segment. Distributed around the globe this species is invasive, thought to be transferred on the hulls of ships.

Bispira sp.
Feather duster worm

This marine polychaete or bristleworm lives in groups with each individual living within its own tube. Inhabiting rocky substrates, each animal has a feather like array of tentacles which it uses to filter the water for plankton.

ARTHROPODA

ARTHROPODA

Arthropoda means jointed leg and includes the insects, spiders and crustaceans. It is the largest of the phylum in the animal kingdom. Species within this phylum have a hard external skeleton, which is periodically shed to allow the animal to grow, and a segmented body. Species within the Crustacea are bilaterally symmetrical with biramous limbs (two branches) and contains the barnacles, shrimps, lobsters and crabs. Their body comprises of a head, thorax and abdomen and they have two pairs of antennae (for touch and smell).

Some crabs use the colour of their carapace to blend with their habitat as in the tidal spray crab *Plagusia depressa* (above), whereas the sponge crab *Dromia* sp. (left) covers its shell with sponge for camouflage

Graspus adscensionis
Ascension sally lightfoot crab
Found along the tide line, mostly out of the water, they move rapidly if disturbed. Juvenile crabs are black to dark brown in coloration and are well camouflaged against the rocks. Adults have beautiful bright red coloration. They feed predominately on algae but they are also scavengers on any dead animals washed ashore. Used as bait by local rock fishermen. Distributed in the eastern Atlantic from the Azores and Morocco to Angola including Ascension and St Helena.

Plagusia depressa
Tidal spray crab

Lives in rocky habitats in tide pools and close to the water surface although it can also be found down to 20m. They are often referred to as rafting crabs due to their habit of clinging to floating debris. Other species of this genus have been recorded to feed predominantly on red coralline algae although also feeding on green seaweeds and also small amphipods. Blue-green in colour with dark red to purple and brown mottling. Distributed in the western Atlantic from Florida, Bahamas, Bermuda, Caribbean, Gulf of Mexico and Brazil, and in the eastern Atlantic from the Azores and Morocco to Angola including Ascension and St Helena.

Percnon gibbesi
Nimble spray crab
or urchin crab

Found in rocky habitats often associated with the black longspined urchin *Diadema ascensionis*, hiding underneath its spines for protection. Although recorded as omnivorous it feeds predominantly on the algae growth covering the rocks. A dark brown flat crab with a distinctive yellow line around its front below its eyes and yellow banding on its legs. Distributed along the Pacific coast of North America and California to Chile, in the western Atlantic from Florida to Brazil and in the eastern Atlantic from the Azores and Morocco to Annobon including Ascension and St Helena. Recently invaded the Mediterranean Sea.

Cryptosoma cristatum
Lesser spotted
shame-faced crab

Lives on sandy substrates usually completely buried to avoid predation. Found in James Bay in 10m and at Egg Island in 20m. Recorded only from the Mediterranean coast of southern Spain, the Azores and St Helena.

Calappa sp.

The bulky shape of its carapace and its flattened claws which fold around to hide its face give these crabs the common name of box crabs or shame-faced crabs. They have a rough well-camouflaged carapace which is covered in many ridges and nodules and often encrusting algae or bryozoans. Usually they are completely buried in sand to hide from large predatory fish and octopus. They feed on gastropod molluscs which live in the sandy habitats and their large strong claws are adapted for cutting open the shells.

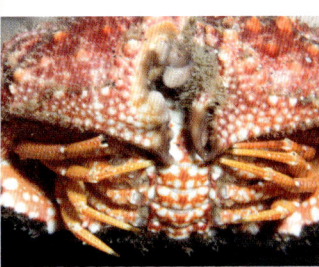

Acanthonyx sanctaehelenae
Decorator crab
Species of *Acanthonyx* can change their carapace colour to match the algae habitat they are living on. It has a pear-shaped carapace which reaches up to 20mm long to tip of rostrum, however specimens collected from Ascension were much smaller. Endemic to Ascension and St Helena.

Pisa sanctaehelenae
St Helena decorator crab
This small (carapace up to 17.9mm long to tip of rostral spine) decorator crab is pale to reddish-brown in colour but is usually covered in small pieces of algae and sponge. Found amongst seaweeds, under rocks and on encrusting ropes, buoys and hulls of ships. Endemic to St Helena.

Paractea rufopunctata africana

Bright to dirty red carapace and legs, often mottled with white on carapace. Carapace has deep grooves between elevated sections and reaches up to 16.3mm in length. Found under rocks or in clumps of coralline algae in depths of 0–45m. Distributed in the central-east Atlantic from Cameroon to the Gulf of Guinea including Ascension and St Helena.

Microcassiope minor

Highly variable in colour including red-brown, pale brown, orange and often with a mottled pattern on the carapace and up to 8.4mm in length. Found under rocks, in tide pools and in clumps of seaweed in depths from the intertidal to 30m (east Atlantic) and c.220m (west Atlantic). Distributed in the western Atlantic from the Bahamas to Venezuela, and in the eastern Atlantic from the western Mediterranean, the Azores to the Gulf of Guinea including Ascension and St Helena.

Pachygraspus loverigei

A small dark brown to olive green crab with white mottling. Carapace length up to 12.9mm. Recorded from near the surface on the buoys at Rupert's Bay and wreck of the Frontier, as well as in James Bay hidden amongst algae on the wreck of the Papa Nui. Endemic to Ascension and St Helena.

Williamstimpsonia denticulatus

This crab varies in colour from white with dark markings to all dark brown or dark orangey-red with dark tips to the claws and numerous marginal teeth on edge of carapace. Carapace length reaches up to 19.8mm. Found in rocky habitat underneath stones or hidden in coralline algae from the intertidal to around 21m. Distributed in the western Atlantic from Bermuda and Bahamas to Brazil and in the eastern Atlantic from Ghana to the Gulf of Guinea including Ascension, St Helena and St Paul's Rocks.

Laleonectes vocans
Insular shore crab

A swimming crab with distinctive paddle-like ends to its fifth pair of legs. Found in depths of 6–309m from the western and central Atlantic. Rare, recorded from two locations at St Helena twice from Long Ledge in 15m and 12m, and once from the wreck of the Darkdale at 33m. Distributed in the western Atlantic from Cuba, Mexico and the Caribbean, and in the eastern Atlantic from Madeira, Cape Verde Islands to Annobon including Ascension and St Helena.

Portunus anceps
Delicate swimming crab

Inhabits sandy areas where it remains completely buried in the sand. Carapace has a mottled sandy coloration providing it with excellent camouflage. The end of its last pair of legs are adapted into paddles which it can use for swimming or burying itself in the sand. It has long thin pincers and a large spine on either side of its carapace for protection against fish predators. Usually in shallow waters down to 20m. Distributed in the western Atlantic from Bermuda and North Carolina to Brazil including Ascension and St Helena.

Dromia sp.
Sponge crab

As its name suggests this crab species carries a sponge on its back for camouflage (often lost in adults). Its last two pairs of legs are modified and positioned on its back so that it can hold the sponge in place. Carapace and claws are covered in fine hairs. Lives on rocky habitats and in caves from 0–100m. Five species of sponge crab are recorded from St Helena: *Metadromia wilsoni*, *Moreiradromia antillensis*, *Dromia erythropus*, *Dromia marmorea* and *Dromia personata*.

Euryozius sangulneus
Blood red crab

Found hidden under rocks from 6–33m. Vivid orange-red carapace with lighter bands on legs and black tips to claws. Endemic to St Helena, Ascension and St Paul's rocks. Often only the empty carapaces found.

Enoplometopus antillensis
Red Atlantic reef lobster
Found in rocky habitats usually
in small crevices and caves, it is
active at night scavenging on both
plant and animal tissue. Bright red
in colour, including antennae, with
white spots on body, white bands
on legs and a distinctive white
circle on either side of its head.
Found in depths from 5–201m.
Grows up to 11cm total length.
Distributed in the western Atlantic
from Bermuda and south-eastern
Florida to Brazil, and in the
eastern Atlantic from Madeira
to the Gulf of Guinea including
Ascension and St Helena.

Panulirus echinatus
Brown spiny lobster

Inhabits caves and under ledges in depths of 0–35m. A nocturnal forager, it is omnivorous, feeding on fish, crustaceans and green and calcareous algae. A highly fecund species with an average of 56,000 eggs per female. Males are generally larger than females reaching up to 39cm body length. Locally called the crayfish or longlegs. Distributed in the Atlantic along the north-eastern coast of Brazil and the Atlantic islands of São Pedro, São Paulo Archipelago, Fernando de Noronha, Rocas Atoll, Trinidad, Ascension, St Helena, Cape Verde and Canary Islands.

Scyllarides obtusus
Red slipper lobster

A nocturnal species, hidden in caves and in crevices during the day, they are seen freely roaming at night in search of mollusc prey, particularly bivalves. Found mostly in depths of 9–75m although reported to migrate to deeper waters during September and October to moult. Locally called the stumpy. Endemic to Ascension, St Helena and Tristan da Cunha.

Dardanus imperator
Hairy hermit crab
or anemone hermit crab

This species has distinctive purple-banded eye stalks and legs, which are also covered in setae (bristles). Often it has anemones on its shell which it uses for protection, especially against octopus predators. In other species of *Dardanus*, the crabs have been seen actively transferring the anemones onto their shells. Found on rocky habitats from 6–30m. Endemic to Ascension and St Helena.

Calcinus tubularis
Stripy-legged hermit crab

This hermit crab varies its shell choice with sex, with most males using normal marine gastropod shells and being able to move around, whereas females usually use empty stationary mollusc shells (for example in the family Vermetidae) and worm tubes which are attached to rocks. It has a blue body with red claws and white eye stalks and has white with red banding on the last segment of each leg. Body length up to 1cm.

Stenopus hispidus
Scarlet-striped
cleaning shrimp or
banded coral shrimp

Found in pairs in crevices and under rocks, the smaller shrimp being the male. They are monogamous and perform a "dance" before mating. A large shrimp (up to 6cm body length) they have a white body with red banding with the body being covered in small spines. As a cleaner shrimp, they wave their white antennae to signal to fish who they clean of parasites and dead flesh.

Lysmata grabhami
White-striped
cleaning shrimp

A beautiful shrimp with two broad red stripes either side of a central white stripe. It usually lives in pairs in crevices or under boulders where it has a cleaner station for fish, removing parasites on which it feeds. Grow up to 6cm. Each shrimp is both male and female at the same time (simultaneous hermaphrodite).

Lysmata spp.
Two new species of shrimp

The blood-red coloured *Lysmata* sp. was found associated with the club-tipped anemone (*Telmatactis*). It has white ends to its red legs, red antennae and the red body has white lines and dots. Recorded on St Helena from Buoys hole and Cavalley Rock. The transparent *Lysmata* sp. has small red dots all over a transparent body which turned blue once put in the tray in the laboratory. Recorded on St Helena from James Bay.

Gnathophylleptum tellei
Telle's bumblebee shrimp

This distinctive shrimp (up to 4cm) has a bright red body with white patches and white head and legs. It is thought to associate with the starfish *Ophidiaster ophidianus* and *Coscinasterias tenuispina*. Recorded only from St Helena (Egg Island at 12m, Red Island, Banks and Rupert's Bay) and the Canary Islands.

Gnathophyllum americanum
Striped bumblebee shrimp

Distributed in circumtropical waters down to 50m depth. Body with thin dark purple/black and white banding, reaching a total length of 3cm. They are carnivores thought to feed on the tube feet of echinoderms on which they are usually found.

Brachycarpus biunguiculatus
Brown-striped shrimp or two claw shrimp

Found in rocky areas it remains hidden in crevices and under rocks during the day. Seen during the night although often hiding under the spines of sea urchins (*Diadema ascensionis*) and quickly retreats under torchlight. Reddish-brown banding on almost translucent body it grows up to 6cm. Claws also have banding and are long although with short slender pincers.

Cinetorhynchus rigens
Atlantic dancing shrimp

Completely hidden during daylight in caves and crevices they are seen usually under rocky ledges at night. When disturbed by torchlight it moves rapidly turning its red and white patterned body, gaining its name "dancing shrimp". Its rostrum is attached to its head by a joint – hence its other name "hinge beaked shrimp". Grows up to 6cm.

Alpheus cedrici
Snapping shrimp
Carapace red to pale red with transverse white band along posterior margin and several colourless or whitish areas on flanks. Abdomen mostly red with whitish patches present near ventral margin of each pleuron. One claw much more developed than the other and if threatened it will "snap" with the larger claw. Found under rocks in 10–15m. Endemic to St Helena and Ascension

Alpheus paracrinitus
Smoothclaw snapping shrimp
A slightly translucent white body with distinctive red bands along the margins of each section of its abdomen. One claw much larger than the other. Lives under small rocks in depths down to 20m. Widely distributed in central Pacific and Indian Oceans as well as central, eastern and western Atlantic.

Janicea antiguensis
Cave shrimp

Inhabits rocky areas especially in caves or under ledges and several individuals have been seen on the wreck of the Frontier at night. Found in depths of 7–20m. A mainly transparent shrimp tinged with red banding, red antennae and white legs. Females have been recorded with numerous small eggs, indicating an extended planktonic larval life, which explains their wide distribution including both the western and eastern Atlantic.

Metapenaeopsis gerardoi
Velvet shrimp

This shrimp is active at night when it can be seen on sandy and muddy bottoms which it inhabits. Its body is translucent and mottled with red, white and brown, giving it good camouflage on the sand. It almost completely buries itself in the sand with often only the eyes being visible.

Thor cf. *manningi*
Anemone shrimp

Lives in association with coral or anemones (particularly the club-tipped anemone *Telmatactis cricoides*) which it uses for protection, as well as feeding on both the tentacle tissue and plankton trapped by the tentacles. It has an orange to reddish-brown body with white bands and spots which are edged with purple blue. Length up to 2cm, with females being larger than males. Also called a "sexy shrimp" as it often holds its tail upwards and waves it around.

Pontonia cf. *pinnophylax*
Fan mussel shrimp

A pair of completely transparent shrimps live within rude pen shells *Pinna rugosa* (pictured left, which are found on cobble or sand patches in rocky areas). The shrimps use the pen shell for protection against fish predators and also feed on organic matter which has been filtered by the pen shell and is attached by mucus to its gills or mantle. Up to 4.5cm long.

Trachycaris restricta

Excellent camouflage makes this species very hard to find; body pink-coloured, like the coralline red algae, and green legs. Found in St Helena at Banks, Munden's Point, and Buttermilk Point on rocky habitat.

Albunea carabus
Mole crab

Lives completely buried on sandy habitats from 0–40m. Distributed in the Mediterranean, eastern Atlantic and St Helena in areas exposed to currents. Dirty white in colour it has an almost rectangular body and all its legs are flattened to aid in digging in the sand. Quickly reburies itself if disturbed. First collected at St Helena by the "Scotia" from James Bay in 1904.

Pseudosquillisma oculata
Mantis shrimp

Mantis shrimp have their second thoracic limb adapted into a raptorial claw making them effective predators and in appearance they look like a praying mantis. They inhabit burrows and predate on shrimps, crabs, molluscs and fish, spearing or smashing their prey with their powerful claws. There are three species of mantis shrimp reported from St Helena, *Alima neptuni*, *Pseudosquilla ciliata* and *Pseudosquillisma oculata*.

Megabalanus azoricus
Giant barnacle

This large barnacle (height up to 5cm) is permanently fixed via the base of its shell to a hard substrate. The opening has two moveable hard plates used for protection, and through here the cirri (adapted legs) are extended. It is a filter-feeder and uses these cirri to trap food particles from the water flowing past. Reproduction is sexual via internal fertilisation from a nearby barnacle and planktonic larvae are released into the water column a few days later.

Balanus trigonus
Pyramid barnacle

This small to medium-sized barnacle reaches a diameter of 2.5cm. Commonest in shallow water, it is found in depths ranging from 1–40m. Native to the Pacific and Indian Oceans it has been introduced to the Atlantic Ocean most likely on ships hulls. Shell has six plates with narrow longitudinal ribs and a pinkish purple tinge.

Lepas anatifera
Common goose barnacle

This barnacle has a clear flexible stalk which it uses to attach itself, often in large numbers, to floating debris, seaweed or to the hulls of ships. Often found washed up at Sandy Bay beach. Its body is protected by five white plates which have black edges and a yellow tip. Its cirri or feeding projections extend outside the plates to capture passing plankton. It has a global distribution found in both tropical and subtropical oceans.

Conchoderma virgatum

This species of stalked barnacle is found attached to sea turtles, whales, fish as well as non-living floating objects. Found on St Helena attached to the FAD (Fish Aggregating Device) off Egg Island. It has a global distribution from polar to tropical seas. It is transparent white in colour with black stripes down the length of its shell and black feeding arms.

BRYOZOA

BRYOZOA

Bryozoans are colonial species often called moss or lace animals. They comprise of a colonial skeleton (made of calcium carbonate or chitin) with chambers which separate individual animals (called zooids), each with a ring of filter-feeding tentacles lined with cilia (small hairs). Some individual zooids are adapted to act as defence or reproductive parts of the colony. Colonies can be encrusting, lacy fans or bushy and can be flexible or rigid. They are predated on by grazing organisms such as sea urchins and fish and can also be subject to competition and overgrowth from sponges, algae, and tunicates. They reproduce by sexual means by producing larva or by the growth of the colony that proceeds asexually.

The distinctive orange edge of the single horn bryozoan *Schizoporella* cf. *unicornis* make it an easy to recognise species. It forms large colonies encrusting boulders

Bugula cf. *dentata*
Dentate moss animal
A tufty blue to light purple colony usually inhabiting vertical rock walls. It is predated on by the green and black nudibranch *Tambja* sp. which uses the secondary metabolites of the bryozoan for its own defence.

Escharoides sp.
An encrusting bryozoan usually found underneath rocks. Pale orange in colour with darker orange edges and large zooids.

Margaretta cf. *levinseni*
Cactus-bush bryozoan
A light orange to straw brown bryozoan with short cylindrical branches with small offshoot branches. Found in depths of 4–20m on rocky habitats.

Membraniporid
Varies in colour from almost translucent white to creamy white with rectangular zooids. Form small to quite large colonies found on the undersides of rocks.

***Schizoporella* cf. *unicornis*
Single horn bryozoan**
Native to Japan, this species is invasive thought to be transported worldwide on ship's hulls. A colonial encrusting bryozoan which is orange when younger becoming dark brown later, although the growing edges remain light orange. Forms large colonies on rocks, preferring shaded areas. Like all bryozoans they are suspension feeders which consume phytoplankton, algae, and bacteria.

MOLLUSCA

MOLLUSCA

Mollusca translates to mean soft body, and this highly diverse group of animals includes the bivalves, snails, octopuses and squids. A large proportion of this phylum have external shells made of calcium carbonate which are secreted from the mantle of the animal. Although there are a great variety of forms, all Mollusca have a mantle, usually in the form of flaps, enclosing the mantle cavity which protects the gills, anus and reproductive pores. They have a well-developed nervous system and most have a radula (rasping tongue) used in feeding.

The class Gastropoda (meaning stomach foot) includes animals with shells (limpets, whelks, winkles, cowries) which secrete a hard shell that grows as the snail does. The soft body has a pair of oral tenticles, and a tubular proboscis (mouth). The foot, or body of the snail is often withdrawn into the shell for protection and often they have a hard "door" called an operculum which is attached to the foot. This class also includes the Opisthobranchs which have a reduced or no external shell (some have small internal shells) and comprises the often very colourful nudibranchs, sea hares, side gill slugs and other sea slugs. Most have a pair of rhinophores on their head (sensory tentacles) and are specialised predators feeding on invertebrates such as sponges and tunicates.

The class Bivalvia have a pair of shells (called valves) protecting the soft body. The valves are hinged together by a ligament and open and close by relaxing and contracting of an abductor muscle. Most are either buried in sand or mud or attached to rocky substrate with byssal threads. They are all filter feeders drawing water in through their siphon and using their large gills to extract oxygen and food particles.

The class Cephalopoda (meaning head foot) includes the squids and octopus. They have eight arms (plus two extra tentacles in squid) with suckers and a powerful beak which tears their prey. They are all carnivores and many have excellent camouflage, changing colour to match their surroundings. They move by jet propulsion, drawing water into their mantle cavity and expelling it quickly.

Molluscs found around St Helena range from the large rude pen shell *Pinna rugosa* (left) to the tiny endemic St Helena mud snail *Nassarius sanctaehelenae* (above right). The white-spotted octopus *Octopus macropus* forages at night out on the sand (below)

Cymbula safiana
Safian limpet
A robust shell with numerous radiating ribs. Inhabits the water line and shallow waters around the coast of St Helena and in rock pools. All limpets are herbivorous and use their radula (rasping tongue) to feed on algae which covers the rocks on which they live. The Safian limpet is distributed in the North Atlantic, Angola, Cape Verde, Mediterranean Sea and St Helena.

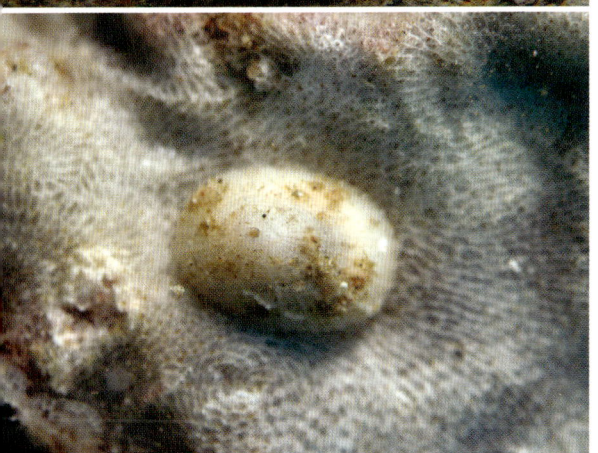

Diodora gibberula
Humped keyhole limpet
An oval-shaped shell with radiating small ribs and with a tiny hole just off centre. The gills are hidden under the edge of the shell and the siphon which encompasses the anus expels waste through the central hole away from the gills. Shell size up to 15mm. Found under rocks. Rare.

Hipponix grayanus
Hoof shell
This limpet-like mollusc is common in St Helena in shallow waters often covering large parts of boulders or bedrock. A creamy white shell which is usually encrusted with algae and grows up to around 14mm. They leave marks on the rocks where they have been.

Echinolittorina helenae
St Helena periwinkle

Intertidal species found clustered in groups in tide pools and crevices in the rock at the high-water mark. Found on St Helena at Manati Bay. A thick straight-sided cone-shaped shell which is pale brown at the top and grey in colour at the bottom. Periwinkles use their radulae to scrape algae from rocks, although some species will also feed on invertebrate larvae.

Echinolittorina punctata

This intertidal species is found in the rock pools and along the tide line at Lot's Wife's Ponds and in James Bay.

Charonia variegata
Atlantic triton trumpet shell

This large mollusc has a pointed shell which is variegated dark brown to cream in colour with a yellow and pale brown patched body. A predatory species it hunts over sandy, gravel and rocky reefs to feed on sea cucumbers and starfish. Reaches a maximum length of 374mm.

Nassarius sanctaehelenae
St Helena mud snail
This marine sea snail is a scavenger, feeding on dead crabs and fish on the muddy or sandy bottoms on which it is found. Often it remains buried in the substrate using its long siphon to detect when food is nearby. It has a white shell with pale to dark brown banding. Height of shell up to 9mm. Endemic to St Helena and Ascension.

Conus jourdani
Globally there are over 600 species of *Conus* but only two species have historically been reported from St Helena, with only this species being found in recent studies. They are a predatory marine gastropod mainly feeding on other marine molluscs and they have a modified radula (tooth) and poisonous venom which they use to paralyse their prey. The shells are often extremely encrusted in coralline algae. On St Helena they are found in reasonable numbers predominately in two areas, Rough Rock and Flagstaff Bay round to Buoy's Hole.

Morula (Morula) consangulnea
This species of rock snail has numerous longitudinal rows of dark brown to almost black nodules and a pointed spire. Relatively rare on St Helena. Reaches a length of up to 14mm.

Stramonita rustica
Rustic rock snail

A solid shell with a large last whorl and nodules in spiral rows which are often well worn. Colour brown to blueish-grey although often overgrown with green or calcareous algae. Shell reaches a total length of 45mm. This species has been found to be an indicator of pollution caused by Tributyltin (TBT) in antifouling paints which induces imposex in the mollusc i.e. the females develop male features including a vas deferens and a penis.

Drillia sinuosa

This white shell has characteristic turret-like sections on the body whorls and fine longitudinal ribs. Reaches a total length of around 25mm.

Coralliophila patruelis
Coral snail

A dirty white-coloured shell with distinctive spiral ribs and angular shoulders to the whorls. Distributed in the Atlantic including St Helena and Barbados.

Mitrella ocellata
White-spotted dove shell
Very common in Lot's Wife's Ponds, they are hidden under rocks during the day and come out at night to feed on algae. Grow up to 14mm in length. An elongated reddish to dark brown shell with numerous white spots.

Cypraecassis testiculus senegalica
Senegal helmet shell
A heavy reddish-brown shell with dark striations and dark stripes over its outer lip. It lives partially buried in the sand during the day, often near rocky reefs. A nocturnal predator they feed on sea urchins. Found in the eastern and western Atlantic from around 10m down to >100m.

Monoplex pilearis
Atlantic hairy triton
This gastropod mollusc has a yellow to orangey-brown shell which is covered in hair-like projections. Its body is white with reddish-brown spots. A predatory species found in rocky habitats in both the eastern and western Atlantic, Indo-Pacific, Cape Verde, Ascension and St Helena.

Bursa corrugata pustulosa
Gaudy frog shell
This predatory mollusc has a reddish to dark brown shell with a large last whorl which has rows of nodules on it. There is a frilled outer edge to the aperture and inside is reddish-brown with white flecks. Often the shell is encrusted with calcareous red algae. Recorded from depths of 2–137m and grows to a maximum size of 75mm.

Polinices lacteus
Milk moon shell
A smooth white shell often with green algal growth. Operculum pale brown. A predatory snail found on sandy and muddy habitats. Reaches a maximum size of 40mm. Recorded in depths from 1–180m.

Notocochlis dillwynii
Zigzag moon shell
A small (up to 14mm) mollusc with a pale brown shell with three distinctive spiral bands of zigzag white and darker brown. Seen at night at Cavalley Rock out foraging on fine sand.

Janthina exigua
Common purple snail
A beautiful fragile light purple shell often found washed up at Sandy Bay beach, sometimes still with their "bubbles". Floats upside down on the ocean surface using air bubbles trapped within a thin layer of chiton. A predatory species feeding on hydrozoans including the purple sail *Velella velella* and the Portuguese man-of-war *Physalia physalis*. Initially all *Janthina* are males, changing sex to females later in life. Maximum width 40mm.

Pyramidella dolabrata

A beautiful smooth white cone-shaped shell with dark brown to almost yellow, thin longitudinal bands. The length of the shell varies between 14mm and 36mm, however only smaller individuals have been seen in St Helena. Distributed in the tropical western Atlantic, West Africa, Indian Ocean, Indo-Pacific region, St Helena, and Ascension in depths from 0–57m. Seen at night on sand at Cavalley Rock.

Melanella atlantica
Atlantic eulimid

A very small (up to approximately 6mm) parasitic mollusc found on the red sea cucumber *Holothuria (Platyperona) sanctori*. Shell is smooth, straight sided, creamy white and conical.

Metaxia rugulosa
Rugged metaxia

A white shell less than 5mm in height which has right-handed shell coiling. Each whorl has three rows of small nodules. Here seen on the slate pencil urchin *Eucidaris tribuloides*.

Luria lurida oceanica
Fallow cowrie

This large cowrie (up to a maximum size of 44mm in length) has a brown dorsal surface with two light bands and two dark dots at each end of its shell. The mantle is dark, almost black. They inhabit rocky areas, hidden under boulders during the day and coming out at night to feed on sponges. Cowries are often preyed upon by octopus and other predatory molluscs. Subspecies endemic to Ascension and St Helena.

Erosaria acicularis sanctahelenae
St Helena cowrie

Dorsally reddish brown with white patternation and distinct darker brown spots around the margins. The mantle is pale brown with numerous small branched protrusions. Nocturnal feeders they are hidden under rocks during the day. Found from shallow water down to 50m. Grows up to 34mm in length. Endemic to Ascension and St Helena.

Cyphoma eludens
Elusive ovulid

A smooth white, elongated solid shell (reaching 31mm in length) with bulbous ends and a 2–3mm dark brown broad band encircling the shell along the margins. The mantle covers the shell and is pale with orange patches. This ovulid has only been found on the black fan coral *Plumapathes pennacea* and fresh feeding traces have been seen on the branches implying that they are true parasites and feed directly on the polyps of their host. They lay transparent egg capsules (3mm diameter with each containing approximately 100–200 larvae) arranged in chains attached to the branches of the host coral.

Cyphoma sp.

Also found on the black fan coral *Plumapathes pennacea*, this Cyphoma has a dark red mantle with white semicircles at its edge. A smaller species, possibly *Pseudocyphoma aureocinctum* (pictured below) had a mottled dark red and white mantle and the shell was much narrower with the bulbous ends not yet developed.

Teredo sp.
Shipworm

This highly adapted mollusc bores holes into wood and secretes chalk to line the bore hole in which it then lives. It has a worm-shaped body and long broad shell. An invasive species it feeds on the wood and by filtering plankton through its siphon. Found in the wood of the wreck of the Portzic.

Vermetid sp.
Worm shell

A solitary sedentary species which lives in an irregularly coiled hard white tube which is permanently adhered to rocky substrate. Tube and operculum often encrusted with algae, tunicates or sponges. Feeds by catching plankton on a mucus net which it secretes. Tube up to approximately 60mm.

Phidiana lynceus
Lynx nudibranch
Body translucent with white line down the middle and orange/pink bands on the oral tentacles and rhinophores. Numerous brown and white cerata on its back. Grows to 30mm, uncommon in St Helena. Predates on hydroids and uses the nematocysts (stinging cells) of the hydroid in its own cerata as a form of protection against predators.

Felimida cf. clenchi
Harlequin blue sea goddess
This beautiful small (<23mm) nudibranch has an orange-brown body with two white patches and numerous pale purple to blueish blotches. The mantle border is yellow and gills and rhinophores are transparent with dark purple lines. Recorded in depths of 0–30m, it is been seen at Buoy's Hole, Bedgellet, Frontier, Half Moon Battery and in James Bay.

Felimida cf. atlantica
Body predominantly white or translucent white with yellowish-orange mantle border and three longitudinal orange stripes, sometimes with further orange spots over body. Rhinophores with white tips and gills transparent with vertical white stripe. They lay eggs on rocks in cream-coloured jelly covered spiral ribbons. Seen on St Helena at Flagstaff Bay, Manati Bay, Egg Island and near the Bedgellet.

***Tambja* sp.**
Green and black nudibranch
Body, gills and rhinophores black with several thick grass-green stripes down either side of its body. Feeds on bryozoans including the blue *Bugula* cf. *dentata*. Found in rocky habitats in depths down to around 20–25m. On St Helena predominantly seen from September to February.

***Felimare* sp.**
Body colour varies from pale to dark blue with three to many golden-yellow lines along their back. Rhinophores are dark blue. Found in rocky and cobble habitats hidden under stones during the day coming out at night to feed on sponges. Spawn in gelatinous white spiral. Size up to 20mm.

Dendrodoris* cf. *angolensis
Dorid
Body predominantly dark purple-brown, mottled with white patches. Smaller individuals have a larger amount of white on body. Dome-shaped body with vein-like pattern to mantle edge. White gills and white tip to rhinophores. Length reported up to 80mm. Recorded in St Helena down to 10m.

Doriopsilla sp.
White-patched nudibranch or painter nudibranch

Pale orange to yellow body, rhinophores and gills. Body has irregular white patches. During the day hide under stones in rocky habitats, roaming at night to feed. Thought to predate on bryozoans, however other species of *Doriopsilla* feed on sponges. Reaching approximately 30mm length in St Helena.

Bornella sp.

White body with orange reticulated pattern. Groups of cerata down either side of body each with cluster of basal gills on the inside of each group. Head with rhinophores on long stalks and star-like oral tentacles. This genus of sea slug feeds exclusively on hydroids. Reaches a total length of around 40mm. Commonly seen in St Helena on rocky habitat from September through to February.

Kaloplocamus ramosus

A small orange species less than 20mm in size with numerous multiple branched processes down each side of the body. Active at night it is reported to feed on bryozoans. Lays eggs in an orange spiralled egg mass. Recorded from Munden's Point and Papa Nui.

Doris cf. *ocelligera*
The body is a translucent dirty white to yellow colour covered in relatively large rounded tubercles which have a darker spot at their tip. Reported to grow up to 25mm, however the one specimen found on St Helena in James Bay was <10mm.

Fiona pinnata
Worldwide distribution. Spends entire life on floating objects in the open ocean such as driftwood and fishing buoys. Feeds on goose barnacles *Lepas anatifera* and floating cnidarians such as *Physalia* and *Velella*. A transparent white body with numerous grey to dark brown irregularly arranged cerata. Grows up to 20mm.

Bulbaeolidia sp.
A chalk-white coloured sea slug with numerous cerata down either side of its body. Red-orange coloration at base of rhinophores. Other species of *Bulbaeolidia* have a weakly kinked white spiral egg mass. Very small reaching a length of 9mm. One specimen recorded on St Helena from Red Boulder Bay near Cat Island.

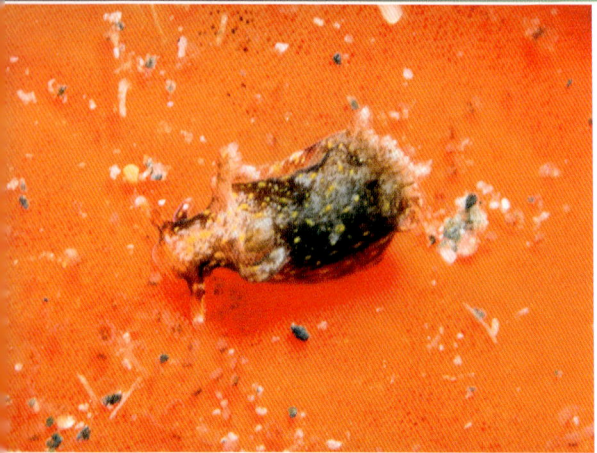

Trapania sp.
Orange volcano sponge sea slug

It is a dark reddish-brown colour with numerous bright yellow markings. Found on the orange volcano sponge (*Tedania* sp.) at night. *Trapania* species feed on Entoprocta, very small animals which live attached to the surface of sponges, bryozoa and hydroids. Reported from St Helena at Cavalley Rock.

Dolabrifera dolabrifera
Sea hare

Found in shallow water and tide pools including Lot's Wife's Ponds. A flattened mottled body with highly variable coloration from white to green to pink. They are herbivores and it is thought possible that their body colour varies depending on the colour of algae they are eating, however this needs further research. Short fused parapodia, long wide oral tentacles and rhinophores. Reach up to 100mm.

Aplysia fasciata
Black sea hare

A slightly mottled olive green-brown to almost black body. It has irregular parapodial flaps on its back which have a pink/purple edge and with which it can swim. Reported to grow up to 400mm, animals seen on St Helena were approximately 250mm. Seen feeding nocturnally on the red algae, harpoon weed *Asparagopsis taxiformis* in shallow water (10m). Sea hares reproduce in pairs, and are famous for also reproducing in chains of many animals, however each individual is both male and female at the same time (simultaneous hermaphrodites). Recorded on St Helena at Roman's reef in July.

Aplysia parvula
Dotted sea hare

A mottled red-brown to olive green body with irregular parapodial flaps on back which cover the mantle cavity in which the shell can be found. Grows up to 60mm. A nocturnal feeder on algae they produce a purple ink (aplysioviolin) if threatened. Spawn is a red string-like gelatinous mass.

Pleurobranchus* cf. *areolatus
Warty side-gilled slug
Body colour varies from creamy white to purple-brown with dark circles. They hide in crevices in the rock or under boulders during the day, coming out at night to feed on sessile invertebrates including sea squirts (ascidians). Reach up to approximately 70mm.

Berthellina* cf. *edwardsi
Peach side-gilled slug
Can vary in colour from pale yellow to bright orange with a smooth slightly transparent body. During daylight they seek refuge beneath rocks, seen out foraging during the night, potentially feeding on sponges. Eggs are laid under stones in loose spiralled pink or white egg masses. A large side-gilled slug they reach up to approximately 70mm in length.

Umbraculum umbraculum
Warty sea umbrella

Body colour variable from white to yellow to orange, covered in numerous large irregular pustules (raised rounded swellings). It has a small, relatively flat, white external shell with an elevated central apex which is usually covered in algal growth. They feed on sponges at night, hidden beneath rocks or buried in sand during the day. Spawn is bright orange or yellow in a frilly oval shape. Grows up to 180mm.

Micromelo undatus
Miniature melo bubble shell

This species has a very light and delicate shell. The minature melo has a white shell (up to 17mm) with three red spiral lines and many sinuous (wavy) longitudinal lines and a translucent to pale blue mantle with white spots and a yellow margin. They feed on cirratulinid polychaete worms, incorporating the worms' toxin for using in its own protection. Recorded in St Helena in tide pools at Manati Bay, Banks and Lot's Wife's Ponds.

Haminoea orbignyana
Bubble shell

A transparent body densely mottled in dark purple/brown. Parapodial lobes are small and fold up over its external shell; however most of the shell is still exposed. Grazes over rocks on diatoms and filamentous algae. Very small reaching maximum length of around 15mm. Seen only at night as it is hidden under rocks during the day.

Pinna rugosa
Rude pen shell

This wedge-shaped bivalve is found partially buried in sand and cobble habitats. It is red brown in colour but usually covered in encrusting life. Its valves have rows of numerous short projections giving it a rough appearance, although in older specimens they are sometimes worn. Within the shell often lives a pair of the fan mussel shrimp *Pontonia* cf. *pinnophylax*. This bivalve reaches a maximum size of 565mm.

Pseudochama cristella
Rock oyster

A bivalve mollusc found strongly adhered to hard substrate, in particular large boulders. Often well camouflaged with algal growth on the shell. The larger right valve is attached to the rock (compared to the left valve in the genus *Chama*) and as they grow the shells curve in a posterior direction. Found in the tropical western Atlantic, the eastern Atlantic islands and St Helena and Ascension.

Pteria hirundo
Wing oyster

Found attached by byssus threads to the black fan coral *Plumapathes pennacea* under ledges and in caves. Often overlooked as it is well camouflaged, with the shell being overgrown with numerous organisms including algae and bryozoans. This bivalve gets its name from a long wing-shaped section of the shell which extends along the valve hinge. Grows up to 110mm.

Lopha cristagalli
Cockscomb oyster

A large bivalve which is attached to rocky substrates, often under ledges or on the roof of caves. Well camouflaged due to the shell being encrusted with bryozoans, algae or sponges. Distinctive zigzag pattern on edge of valves where they interlock. A suspension feeder extracting nutrients by filtration from the seawater.

Limaria hians
File clam
This bivalve has a white shell with radiating ribs and pale pink to bright orange tentacles. Moves in a pulsating motion by repeatedly opening and closing its shell. It is relatively common hidden under rocks within an area of small stones and shell fragments which it has bound together with sticky byssus threads to form a "nest".

Arca bouvieri
Ark clam
There are around 200 species of ark clam globally, distinguished by the long straight hinge between their two valves. *Arca bouvieri* is relatively large (up to approximately 80mm long) and has radiating ribs. The shell is a creamy white colour but is often overgrown by coralline algae.

Acar domingensis
White miniature ark clam
A small (<25mm length) bivalve that lives under stones, small rocks or boulders, usually in reasonable numbers. Found from North Carolina to West Indies, Cape Verde Islands and at St Helena and Ascension.

Bractechlamys corallinoides
Coral scallop

Eight to ten thick ribs are present on the fan-shaped valve some with small lumps. Ears of valve are unequal in size. They can swim through the water to avoid predators by creating a jet propulsion from opening and closing the two valves together. Rows of simple blue eyes are situated on the edge of the mantle.

Pecten sp.
Atlantic scallop

A filter-feeding bivalve with much smoother radiating ribs than *Bractechlamys corallinoides*. Rare on St Helena, with solitary individuals being found under ledges or in crevices on the Frontier, Billy May's Revenge and Egg Island. Valves are often encrusted with algae, sponges or tunicates. Ears of valve are unequal in size.

Euvola turtoni

The smallest of the scallop species found on St Helena with the valves having a total length of approximately 3cm. One valve is flattened whilst the other is slightly convex with valves with equal sized ears. Shell varies from mottled pale pink and white to a dusky darker pink. Found in sandy habitats, they are filter feeders.

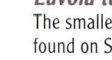

Americardia media
Heart-shaped bivalve or Atlantic strawberry cockle

A white to cream bivalve with pinkish-red mottling, it gets its name from the heart shape the two valves make. Reaches a maximum total length of 35mm. Distributed in the western Atlantic from the south-east of North America to Brazil, Ascension and St Helena in depths of 0–140m.

Semele modesta

A white bivalve which has distinctive concentric rings. Relatively common on St Helena in sandy areas. Common shell width approximately 30mm. Distributed throughout the islands of the Gulf of Guinea, coast of central West Africa, St Helena and Ascension.

Tellina mexicana

This bivalve inhabits sandy areas where it buries itself beneath the surface. Water and food are drawn down to the mollusc through a siphon and it is a filter feeder. The shell is white with variable colour patterns including red, yellow or grey. It has numerous ribs radiating from the hinge. Reaches a total length of around 80mm.

Octopus occidentalis
Common octopus

A very well-camouflaged species with highly variable coloration from reddish-brown to dark purple-brown, although they will quickly change colour to pale beige if frightened. Predates on crustaceans and molluscs; the shells of which are often deposited around its den. It releases a nerve poison in its saliva which paralyses prey and it uses its beak to drill holes in the shells of its prey. Reaches a maximum total length of 130cm. Inhabits rocky areas from 1–200m. Females produce numerous (up to 400,000) small eggs (<2mm) which it lays in rock crevices and then guards until they hatch. Locally taken for food and referred to as catfish.

Octopus macropus
White-spotted octopus

Found on sandy and cobble habitats the white-spotted octopus has a reddish-brown body with white spots. Body length 60mm, arm length 150mm. It predates on shrimps and crabs. Both juveniles and adults seen at Cavalley Rock. Circumglobal distribution in warm to temperate waters in depths of 5–100m.

Tremoctopus violacea
Blanket octopus

This pelagic octopus is named for the large transparent webs of tissue which connects several of the arms and is used as a defence mechanism to make the animal look much larger. The webs are only found in adult females which reach a size of 200cm, the males are much smaller reaching just over 2cm. The males and small immature females use the poisonous tentacles of Portuguese man-of-war *Physalia physalis* for defence and to capture prey.

ECHINODERMATA

ECHINODERMATA

All species of Echinoderms are marine and as their name suggests they have a "spiny skin" covering their hard internal skeleton. They are distinguished by their body having radial symmetry, usually with five sections. Most have numerous tube feet or podia which are filled with fluid and are used in locomotion, as sensory organs or as a means to catch food. There are around 7,000 living species of echinoderms worldwide with 43 species recorded to date in the waters around St Helena.

Long-armed starfish *Chaetaster longipes*

Black longspined urchins *Diadema ascensionis* are more active at night when they come out to feed

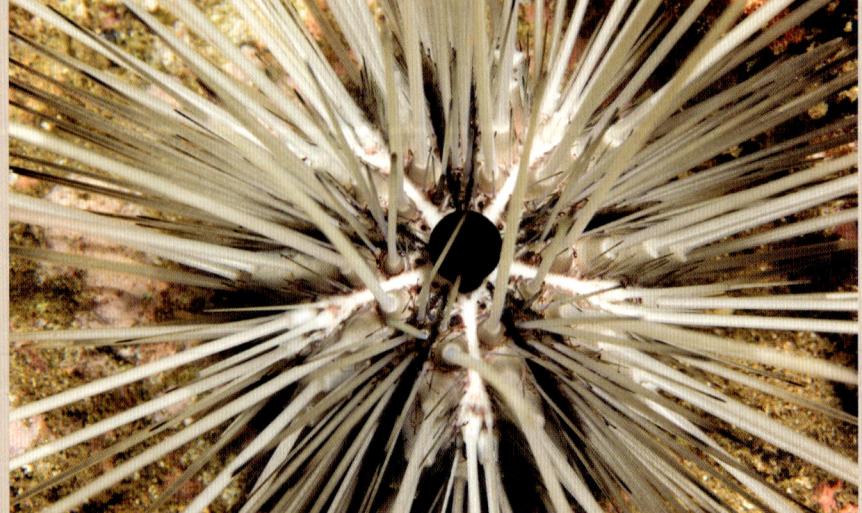

Holothuria (Platyperona) sanctori
Red sea cucumber

A nocturnal species found on rocky habitats. They are dark reddish-brown in colour and are relatively common. If attacked or disturbed they release white sticky threads which release a poison and entangle would-be predators. Reproduction is annual with a high-intensity seasonal spawning event followed by a rest period. They feed on detritus and play an important role in the ecosystem in recycling nutrients.

Holothuria (Thymiosycia) arenicola
Sand sea cucumber

A circumtropical species of sea cucumber which inhabits sandy areas, usually completely buried in the sand. They are difficult to find without digging In the sand, therefore only a few individuals have been recorded to date including from Cavalley Rock. Coloration is light brown/tan with dark brown patches. A detritus feeder. IUCN Red Listed as Data Deficient.

Euapta lappa
Yellow-banded sea cucumber

A long (up to 100cm) grey-white body with yellow stripes and knobbly appearance. Fifteen feathery tentacles are used to feed on detritus. Body is covered in tiny hooks which make it feel sticky to touch. A nocturnal species it remains hidden under rocks during the day. It is a highly contractile species which uses the contraction of the body wall muscles to move. Inhabits depths down to 30m.

Tropiometra carinata
Black and white sea lily

A variety of colour morphs exist from black to yellow-brown to variegated black and white.
This feather star is the dominant invertebrate in St Helena's inshore rocky habitats. Their ten arms protrude from many rock cracks and crevices and they use their numerous basal cirri to hold fast to the rocks. A circumtropical species found along the South African coast they live to depths of 40m. They feed by trapping floating planktonic particles with their arms and then bringing the items to their central mouth. They can swim if disturbed and will use their cirri to move along rocks to better feeding areas.

Coscinasterias tenuispina
Eight-armed starfish
Colour varies from blue to green to brown and they are often well camouflaged. It is an omnivore feeding on bivalve molluscs and other echinoderm species. It reproduces both sexually (usually in winter) and asexually (usually in summer). Asexual reproduction occurs by dividing in half, hence it is often seen with several legs much shorter than the others. Usually it has eight arms, however individuals with between 4–10 arms are also seen. Grows up to 27cm and inhabits rocky and sandy habitats from a few metres down to 50m.

Ophidiaster ophidianus
Purple sea star
With five tubular arms this species has highly variable colour, including orange, red and dark purple, and often with a mottled appearance. Maximum size 40cm though predominately 15–20cm. It is found on rocky habitats where it feeds on algae and detritus. Lives in depths to 100m though commonly less than 20m.

Parvulastra exigua
Variable cushion star
This small cushion star has a pentagonal-shaped body with no distinctive arms and has a variegated colour, including green, blue, orange and pale brown. It is found mainly in the intertidal area in rock pools including Lot's Wife's Ponds and Lemon Valley where it feeds on algae. Distribution includes St Helena, South Africa and southern Australia.

Astropecten sanctaehelenae
St Helena sea star
Found in sandy habitats, often completely buried. A dusky pink-coloured body with five rigid tapered arms. Arms are bordered with 25–26 marginal plates down each side, each with large white spines. Recorded from depths of 20–60m. Sand stars of the genus *Astropecten* are predators of molluscs, worms, crustaceans, and other echinoderms. Endemic to St Helena.

Astropecten variegatus
Variegated sea star
This species inhabits sandy areas, often completely buried. A variegated dark brown and creamy-yellow coloured body with five rigid tapered arms. Arms are bordered with 15–16 marginal plates down each side, each with small spines. Recorded from depths of 20–50m. A predator of molluscs, worms, crustaceans, and other echinoderms. Endemic to St Helena and Ascension.

Tethyaster magnificus
Sand star

A large bright orange starfish with five arms, each with a conspicuous border of whiteish spines. Found in soft sandy habitats completely buried in the sand, a star-shaped mound giving away their position. They are a voracious predator with their mouth found on their lower surface. Species in the genus *Tethyaster* are some of the top carnivores in the food web feeding on other echinoderms and molluscs, and as would be expected for such predators, their population density is very low. Endemic to St Helena and Ascension.

Luidia sagamina
Dark red sand star

Dorsally a reddish-brown coloration with a conspicuous border to each of the five long arms of numerous creamy-white spines. They inhabit sandy areas where they bury themselves completely during the day, coming out at night to forage. Thought to have a worldwide distribution due to its long planktonic larval stage. Found from 15–50m. Recorded in St Helena at Cavalley Rock. Longest arm around 13cm however readily sheds arms as a defence mechanism.

Ophiothrix roseocaerulans
Common brittlestar
A very common species intertidally and in shallow waters under stones and rocks, although also recorded down to 55m. Colour varies from almost black to dark purple to lightest pink (although darker colours are more predominant). *Ophiothrix* diet mainly comprises of organic matter, detritus and phytoplankton. Endemic to St Helena and Ascension.

Eucidaris tribuloides
Slate pencil urchin
Found in rocky habitats, wedged under rocks and in crevices during the day. Comes out at night to feed on sponges, algae, corals and bryozoans. They have thick blunt spines which are often covered in encrusting algae or other organisms. Two morphs seem to exist, one with short fat spines the other with longer thinner spines. Distributed in both eastern and western Atlantic.

Pseudoboletia atlantica
Hairy pincushion urchin
Found under boulders, it often covers itself in stones and algae. Colour white to cream, although it can be greenish and sometimes it has banded spines. Found at 10m in James Bay, and historically dredged off Manati Bay in 20m. Other species of *Pseudoboletia* feed on algae and small invertebrates. Endemic to St Helena and Ascension.

Diadema ascensionis
Black longspined urchin

A predominantly black, although occasionally white, sea urchin which has numerous sharp long thin spines. It is relatively common on rocky habitats but is hidden, wedged in crevices or under rocks, during the day. They are nocturnal grazers seen moving around in the open at night feeding on algae. Endemic to St Helena and Ascension.

Echinometra lucunter
Rock boring urchin

This elliptical shaped black sea urchin has much shorter, thicker spines than *Diadema ascensionis* and it is found in shallow water and in intertidal areas. It gets its name from its ability to use its teeth to bore holes in the rocks. It then uses these holes to hide in during the day and protect itself from predators. It comes out into the open at night to feed on algae. Distributed in the western Atlantic, Caribbean Sea, Ascension and St Helena.

Brissus unicolor
Grey heart urchin
Found on sandy habitats completely buried in the sand. A large grey urchin (test up to 13cm) covered in small soft spines. The empty test (shell of dead animal) has a distinctive almost turtle shell like pattern.

Echinocardium connectens
St Helena burrowing urchin
Its irregular oval shape means *Echinocardium* species are often referred to as heart urchins. It is covered in small creamy white spines, with specialised spines underneath used for burying itself completely in sand. Other species of *Echinocardium* are reported to feed on detritus. Recorded from St Helena off Egg Island in sandy habitat. Endemic to St Helena.

Echinoneus cyclostomus
Little burrowing urchin
[not illustrated]
A small sea urchin which burrows in the sand and is a deposit feeder. Alive it is reported to be deep red to pale brown in coloration. Distributed from East Africa to Hawaii (including the Hawaiian Islands), in the tropical Indo-Pacific Ocean and western Atlantic. Recorded from depths 0–120 m.

CHORDATA: ASCIDIACEA

CHORDATA: ASCIDIACEA

Related to vertebrates, Ascidiacea belongs to the tunicates which are highly advanced animals, having a tail, dorsal nerve cord and notochord at some point in their life (especially evident when larvae). Sea squirts or benthic tunicates are sedentary and are attached to rocky substrates, cobbles or free individuals anchored to sediment by rhizoids. They have inhalant and exhalant siphons used to pump water (carrying oxygen and food particles and removing waste) through their body. The siphons can be quickly closed if the animal is disturbed. Their body is enclosed in a cellulose tunic and they are often vibrantly coloured. Sea squirts can be either solitary or colonial, comprising of numerous zooids which either have their own siphons or share exhalant siphons.

Ascidians can be quite well camouflaged like the dome-shaped *Polyclinum costellatum* (above) or brightly coloured like *Symplegma rubra* (left)

Ascidia sp.

A solitary transparent ascidian found attached to the underside of rocks. Size approximately less than 50mm.

Polycarpa sp.
(gr. *P. spongialis*)

A solitary dark purple ascidian with two large protruding siphons. Body often camouflaged by encrusting algae. Found in rocky crevices and under ledges.

Styelidae sp.

A solitary ascidian with single inhalant and exhalant siphons. Red or orange in colour with a rough wrinkled external appearance. Several were found on rocks in a cave at Buttermilk Point.

Symplegma cf. *viride*
Encrusting social tunicate
Bright yellow individuals with separate siphons are attached at their base to form a colony, often covering a large area of rock.

Symplegma rubra
A vivid red colonial ascidian, usually found under rocks and artificial structures in inshore waters. Common in south-eastern Brazil, it is distributed throughout the western Atlantic as well as off Tanzania, Mozambique and in St Helena. Colonies can reach more than 40cm in diameter.

Symplegma brakenhielmi
A colonial ascidian with 3mm bright pink individual zooids, each with two siphons on the surface of the colony. The zooids are embedded in a common and translucent thin tunic.

***Didemnum* sp.**
A thin white colonial sea squirt with numerous small inhalant siphons and fewer, larger shared cloacal openings, where the exhalant siphons flow.

***Polysyncraton* sp.**
An orange encrusting colonial sea squirt recorded from Lot's Wife's Ponds. As for other members from family Didemnidae, numerous small inhalant siphons are present with fewer, larger cloacal openings that share exhalant siphons.

Polycitoridae sp.
Several small zooids embedded in a common purple-blue coloured tunic.

Polyclinum costellatum
A colonial tunicate found in various colours including red and dark green. With a jelly-like consistency it forms a dome-shamed mound. The zooids are arranged in star-like patterns around large cloacal openings.

CHORDATA: CHONDRICHTHYES

CHORDATA: CHONDRICHTHYES

Fish in the class Chondrichthyes have their skeleton made of cartilage rather than bone. They include the sharks and rays and all species within this group have jaws. Sharks and rays lack scales but instead have a tough skin which feels rough like sandpaper due to tooth-like denticles which are used for protection and in some cases streamlining. They breathe through gill slits (usually 5–7 slits) and ensure the flow of oxygenated water over their gills either by swimming or they pump the water through a spiracle (a small hole near their eye) and out over their gills.

Several pelagic Chondrichthyes species are found around St Helena including the blue shark *Prionace glauca* (above) and the Chilean devil ray *Mobula tarapacana* (left)

Rhincodontidae

Rhincodon typus
Whale shark

Whale sharks are grey dorsally to light grey underneath with numerous white spots, the configuration of which can be used to identify individuals. This largest species of fish can reach lengths of up to 14m. They give birth to live young. Diet consists mainly of plankton, filter feeding through their large mouths (to 1.5m wide) though they will also take small fish. This migratory species has an IUCN Red List status of Vulnerable. Seasonal around St Helena from November to May.

The following other species of shark have been recorded in the waters around St Helena: Alopiidae – *Alopias superciliosus* **bigeye thresher**; Lamnidae – *Isurus oxyrinchus* **shortfin mako** (occasionally caught as bycatch); Carcharhinidae – *Prionace glauca* **blue shark**, *Carcharhinus galapagensis* **Galapagos shark**, *Carcharhinus longimanus* **oceanic whitetip shark**; Sphyrnidae – *Sphyrna* sp. **hammerhead**, *Pseudocarcharias kamoharai* **crocodile shark**, Hexanchidae – *Notorynchus cepedianus* **sevengill cowshark**.

Myliobatidae

Mobula tarapacana
Chilean devil ray

Although predominately an oceanic species it is also found in coastal waters reaching a maximum disc width of 370cm. Presumed circumglobal in tropical waters. It only has one working ovary (left side) and produces one pup per litter, reproduction being aplacental viviparity (eggs hatch inside mother and given birth to as live young). This large devil ray is dark olive green to brown on the dorsal side with short head fins which it uses for catching small fish and crustaceans found in the plankton. The tail is shorter than the disc and lacks a spine. The ventral surface is white with a distinctive grey pattern. Tagging studies have found devil rays to travel distances up to 3,800km and dive to depths of over 1,800km.

CHORDATA: ACTINOPTERYGII

CHORDATA: ACTINOPTERYGII

Fish in this class have only a single gill slit on each side of their head and a bony skeleton. Their fins comprise of bony spines with webs of skin between giving them the name ray finned fish. This is a very diverse group of vertebrate with an amazing array of colours, shapes and sizes and occupying a range of habitats from the open ocean to the deep sea to inshore sandy areas and rocky reefs. There are 156 species recorded from around St Helena with 9 species found only on St Helena and another 16 species endemic to St Helena and Ascension.

The most abundant and one of the most beautiful species around St Helena is the endemic St Helena butterflyfish *Chaetodon sanctaehelenae* forming shoals into their thousands

The endemic St Helena damselfish
Chromis sanctaehelenae

Damselfish eggs are laid on the surface of boulders and are guarded by the male

Muraenidae

Muraena pavonina
Whitespot moray
A single specimen reported by a fisherman in St Helena. Generally they are present in shallow water although have been found down to 60m. Body is pale grey/light brown with numerous white spots and a distinctive black spot around the gill opening. Tropical distribution both in western and eastern Atlantic. Found in holes between rocks and in crevices, coming out at night to feed. They are thought to be born female changing sex at some point in their life after spawning to become males (protogynous hermaphrodites).

Enchelycore anatina
Fangtooth moray
Predators of small fish and crustaceans, the fangtooth moray remains generally well hidden in crevices and among rocks waiting for its prey to pass by. Found in depths of 3–60m they grow to a total length of 120cm. Dark brown in coloration with a yellow/white mottled pattern which varies with age.

Enchelycore carychroa
Caribbean chestnut moray
A small olive brown moray reaching a maximum total length of 34cm. It inhabits rocky areas hidden under boulders in depths of 1–20m. Seen at night on Roman's reef. Distributed in the western Atlantic, Ascension and St Helena.

Gymnothorax miliaris
Goldentail moray
The colour of this species makes it easily recognisable with its dark brown body and numerous yellow spots. Some individuals can be the reverse with a predominately bright yellow body. They reach a maximum length of 70cm but commonly 40cm. It is found in depths of 0–60m though usually 0–35m. This species will forage in the open during daylight, but usually it is seen hiding amongst rocks. *Gymnothorax vicinus* **purplemouth moray** is also reported from around St Helena.

Gymnothorax moringa
Spotted moray

This subtropical species is found down to depths of 200m but is very common in shallow water (0–35m). Usually hidden amongst rocks but also seen free swimming in the open. Care should be taken as this species has been known to attack divers. It is active during the day and forages on both fish and crustaceans. A white/pale yellow body with dark purple/brown spots covering the whole body. It is a large moray eel reaching 200cm (generally 60cm). Common around St Helena it is taken by local fishermen for food (locally called the conger).

Gymnothorax unicolor
Brown moray

Uniformly brown in coloration with a blunt snout this moray eel reaches a maximum length of 100cm. It predates on small crabs and gastropods and lives in rocky/ boulder areas hiding in crevices and holes. Two individuals have been seen fighting, presumably over a territorial dispute. Distribution is subtropical throughout the eastern Atlantic and also in the Mediterranean. This species is eaten by locals on St Helena and is commonly called the Greek.

Congridae

Ariosoma mellissii
Melliss's conger

The presence of distinct pectoral fins distinguish this as a conger eel (as opposed to moray eels which lack pectoral fins). It has a scaleless pale grey/tan coloured body with large eyes. Reaches a total length of 50cm. Seen at night on sand, usually buried with only the head being visible. If disturbed it completely buries itself tail first. Recently seen at Munden's Point, Cavalley Rock, Roman's reef and historically reported from Egg Island and Flagstaff Bay. Endemic to St Helena.

Ophichthidae

Ophichthus regius
Ornate snake eel

A pale brown eel covered in large and smaller dark brown spots. Records of this species from Grattan seamount, 260km south-east of Ascension Island. Endemic to Ascension, St Helena and St Paul's Rocks. Inhabits sandy areas of the continental shelf where it buries itself in the sand. Maximum reported total length 90cm.

Synodontidae

Synodus synodus
Diamond lizardfish

They get their name from the dark regular diamond pattern down the length of their body and their head being shaped like a lizard. Generally pale beige to sand coloured although some smaller fish can be pale red in colour. Well camouflaged they are found on rocky substrates down to 90m (common to 35m). They lie motionlessly in wait for passing prey (usually small fish) which they catch with their many sharp teeth. Have been seen to prey on the St Helena butterflyfish. Commonly 20cm total length, they can reach a maximum length of 33cm.

Trachinocephalus myops
Bluntnose lizardfish
or snakefish

Predominantly found buried in the sand often with only their head showing, waiting for unsuspecting fish or crustaceans to predate upon. They have a blunt nose, upturned mouth and are blue/grey in colour with alternate pale blue and gold stripes with black edges. Found down to 400m but usually 3–90m and reaching a maximum total length of 40cm. Distributed worldwide in tropical and temperate waters.

Antennariidae

Frogfish

Two species of frogfish have been reported from St Helena *Antennarius nummifer* and *Antennarius striatus*. Variable colour from brown to orange with coloured blotches and several filaments on head and body. Three individuals have been recorded recently, at night in James Bay at 8m, on the Frontier in 20m and at Long Ledge in 18m. Very well camouflaged, they sit motionless waiting for passing crustaceans or small fish, enticing them close to their mouth with a "lure" which is actually a modified first dorsal spine.

Exocoetidae

Flyingfish

There are five species of flyingfish recorded in St Helena waters: *Cheilopogon nigricans* African or blacksail flyingfish, *Cheilopogon pinnatibarbatus* Bennett´s flyingfish (pictured left), *Exocoetus obtusirostris* Oceanic two-wing flyingfish, *Exocoetus volitans* tropical two-wing flyingfish and *Hirundichthys speculiger* mirrorwing flyingfish. Flyingfish use their enlarged pectoral fins to glide large distances over the surface of the water to escape predators including tuna, marlin and dolphins. They have a strongly forked tail fin with elongated lower lobe which they use for propulsion. Flyingfish are omnivores mainly feeding on plankton.

Belonidae

Platybelone argalus trachura
Ascension keeled needlefish

Endemic to Ascension and St Helena, this silver fish has a slender elongated body with a needle-like beak. They swim and hunt in shoals in coastal waters near the surface at a depth of around 2m. Other species of this genus feed mainly on small fish and have pelagic eggs. Maximum total length 50cm.

Holocentridae

Holocentrus adscensionis
Squirrelfish

Pinkinsh-red in colour with silver/white patches and a yellow dorsal fin. Squirrelfish have a sharp spine on their gill cover and sharp dorsal fin rays. Relatively common down to 35m this species generally hides under ledges and overhangs during the day, although also seen in the open over cobble and sand habitats. A nocturnal species which feeds on small crustaceans it can be found singly or in large groups. Maximum size up to 61cm total length. This species is fished locally for food and referred to as the hardback soldier.

Myripristis jacobus
Blackbar soldierfish

A bright red fish with a distinctive black bar across its gill cover and white edges to its fins. Its large eyes are indicative of its nocturnal behaviour, feeding mainly on planktonic species. Found in caves and under ledges generally down to 35m, although it does occur to depths of 100m. This subtropical species is taken occasionally for food and locally called the softback soldier. Maximum total length 25cm.

Aulostomidae

Aulostomus strigosus
Trumpetfish or Atlantic cornetfish

Pale brown in coloration (although xanthochromic yellow morphs are occasionally seen) with a dark tail with three white stripes. This fish is often seen hanging vertically in the water column, sometimes in caves. Distributed in the eastern Atlantic this species is found in depths of 2–25m where it predates on shrimps and small fish.

Syngnatidae

Hippocampus sp.
Seahorse

Pale brown to pinkish in colour they are well camouflaged. Seahorses are scaleless, their body comprising of body plates. Female seahorses deposit up to 1,500 eggs in the brood pouch of the males, where they stay until they are fully developed. They feed on small crustaceans including copepods and shrimp. On St Helena they have been found in the stomachs of tunas by fishermen. Single individuals have been sighted in 10m at Buoys Hole and in Rupert's Bay at 13m.

Scorpaenidae

Pontinus nigropunctatus
St Helena deepwater scorpionfish

A deepwater species found in depths of 130–183m. Body is pale orange with numerous yellow spots all over and some darker brown spots on its dorsal surface. Individuals up to a maximum total length of 42.5cm have been recorded. Endemic to St Helena (including being caught at Bonaparte seamount) and St Paul's Rocks. This fish is eaten locally and referred to as the deepwater jack.

Scorpaena mellissii
Melliss's scorpionfish

Endemic to St Helena. A variable mottled coloration from red to orange-red and the fins have a striking pattern of brown-coloured spots. Usually seen at night, it inhabits shallow water from 10m on rock, on sand and in crevices and can occasionally be found to depths of 110m. Like other members of the scorpionfish family they are carnivorous predating on small fish and crustaceans, lying motionless they use their excellent camouflage to surprise prey. They also have venomous spines which can be very painful if touched. Grows to at least 23cm standard length.

Scorpaena plumieri
Spotted scorpionfish

This species has excellent camouflage and lies motionless on rocky or sometimes sandy bottoms. Found in depths from 5–55m it reaches a maximum total length of 45cm. It predates predominantly on fish and crustaceans. When disturbed the white spots on a black area on the base of the pectoral fin can be clearly seen. They have a venomous spine on their foredorsal fin which can cause severe pain to humans if touched.

Scorpaenodes insularis
Ascension scorpaenodes

Endemic species to Ascension Island, St Helena and St Paul's Rocks. Occurs from 3–35m on rocky substrate, usually hidden in crevices or caves. More conspicuous at night this small fish (up to 10cm standard length) is bright red in colour with numerous white spots. They remain motionless on the bottom waiting for passing prey which is usually small fish or crustaceans.

Serranidae

Epinephelus adscensionis
Rock hind

Inhabiting rocky areas this usually solitary fish predates predominately on crabs and small fish. It has been caught down to depths of 120m but is common in waters less than 35m. It has numerous dark reddish spots all over a tan body but can also be darker in colour. All individuals start life as females transforming to males at approximately 5 to 8 years of age (protogynous sexual development). It has been recorded to live to over 16 years. A common species taken inshore by local rock fishermen and referred to as the jack.

Holanthias fronticinctus
St Helena seaperch

Although locally called the deepwater greenfish it is actually a beautiful yellow-orange colour, with two purple bands on the head and around the dorsal fin. At a size of around 20–21cm the females change sex to males (as in other species in this family) and their morphology changes, in particular the fins get larger. It can be occasionally caught in depths of about 110m. Endemic to St Helena and Grattan seamount (260 km south-east of Ascension Island). Attains a size of at least 22cm.

Rypticus saponaceus
Greater soapfish

A solitary species, the soapfish can produce poisonous soapy mucus from its skin to deter predators. Inactive during the day they are usually hidden under ledges lying on their side, however at night they are swift predators feeding on small fish especially cardinalfish. They are a mottled grey to brownish-grey in colour, often with a white stripe down the top of their head, and they reach up to 32cm total length. Widespread distribution in the tropical Atlantic.

Serranus sanctaehelenae
St Helena comber

(not illustrated)
Locally called the deepwater brown mullet this species is endemic to St Helena and Ascension. It has a pale brown-coloured body with usually six dark bars. It reaches a total length of 21cm. It is caught by fisherman at depths of about 110m.

Priacanthidae

Cookeolus japonicus
Longfinned bullseye
This red to silvery coloured fish has a distinctive long pelvic fin and reaches a maximum total length of 69cm (commonly 30cm). Found in deepwater 40–400m (usually 165–200m) over rocky substrates in the tropical regions of the Indo-Pacific, eastern Pacific, western Atlantic and at St Helena. Predates on pelagic crustaceans.

Heteropriacanthus cruentatus
Glasseye snapper
These nocturnal fish live in caves or under ledges, either on their own or in small groups. They feed on shrimps, small larval fish, crabs and polychaetes. Relatively common this species can be found from 5–35m and are circumtropical in distribution. Their colour varies from deep red to a pale silvery-pink and they have an upturned mouth. Considered a local delicacy this fish is locally referred to as bullseye. Size up to 50cm.

Apogonidae

Apogon axillaris
Axillary-spot cardinalfish

These small red fish have a black dot on the base of their pectoral fin. Juveniles are almost transparent and often seen at night on sand. They have large eyes and are nocturnal, found hiding in caves and in crevices during the day. Endemic to Ascension and St Helena. Maximum size 15cm and common in depths of 4–35m. Male cardinalfish brood their young in their mouths.

Echeneidae

Remora albescens
White suckerfish

Uniform white to pale grey in coloration with a sucking disc on its head to attach to the host. Usually host specific to manta or devil rays though has been seen on whale sharks and rarely on black marlin. Sometimes found within the gill cavity or mouth of the host species. Circumtropical distribution in warm seas they grow to maximum standard length of 30cm.

Remora remora
Sharksucker

Coloration is dark brownish grey sometimes with speckling. Reaches a maximum size of 86cm though commonly 40cm. This species is usually associated with sharks though also found on turtles, large fish and also free swimming. It will feed on parasites of the host species (e.g. parasitic copepods). Distributed in warm circumglobal waters.

There are two other species of remora also reported from St Helena, **Remora osteochir marlinsucker** caught attached to a white marlin and **Echeneis naucrates live sharksucker** which is found usually attached to sharks or sunfish.

Carangidae

Caranx crysos
Blue runner

A carnivorous silver fish of the jack family which feeds on pelagic fish, shrimps and other crustaceans. It is highly streamlined and has body plates (called scutes) on the straight part of its lateral line near its tail. It has a dark spot on the edge of its operculum in line with its eye and it has a falcate (sickle-shaped) pectoral fin. Forming schools in depths of 0–100m it reaches a maximum total length of 70cm and has been reported to live up to 11 years. It spawns offshore and has pelagic eggs. IUCN Red Listed status as Least Concern.

Caranx lugubris
Black jack

This circumtropical dark grey to black-coloured jack is found in depths of 12–354m generally in oceanic waters but occasionally inshore at reef edges and drop-offs. It has a distinctive high forehead and reaches a total maximum length of 100cm. A nocturnal predator it feeds on small fish. Usually solitary it sometimes forms schools. Eggs are pelagic.

Caranx ruber
Bar jack

A streamlined silver fish with a distinctive blue line with a black line above it along the top of its back from its head down to its lower tail. Distributed in the western Atlantic and West Indies its maximum reported total length is 69cm (commonly 50cm). Rarely seen in St Helena, this species feeds on fish and small invertebrates.

Decapterus punctatus
Round scad

A shoaling species found in shallow water less than 10m. It is found in tropical and subtropical waters from the western and eastern Atlantic including Ascension and St Helena. Predates on copepods and other zooplankton. Round scad spawn their pelagic eggs year round in offshore waters. They are caught commercially and used as bait in the tuna pole and line fishery.

Decapterus macarellus
Mackerel scad

(not illustrated)
A pelagic fish which forms large fast-moving shoals which feed on zooplankton. It has a slender elongated silver body with a blueish or greenish sheen and a dark spot on its operculum. Attains a total maximum length of 46cm. Seasonal to St Helena, it is used as a bait fish for tuna fishing when found in large numbers.

Decapterus muroadsi
Yellowtail mackerel or stonebrass scad

Used as bait fish by commercial tuna fishermen, it is also eaten by locals. The yellowtail mackerel is common in large shoals around dusk and dawn in inshore waters. A silver fish with distinctive yellow upper lobe to its tail. These pelagic fish prey predominately on planktonic invertebrates and are commonly around 30cm fork length.

Decapterus tabl
Roughear scad or redtail scad

A plankton feeder taking mostly copepods, this species forms large schools. Taken by local fishermen around Speery Ledge, large shoals of juveniles have also been seen around the stern of the Papa Nui. Reaching a fork length of around 40cm this silver species has a red tail and has a dark blue dorsal coloration.

Elagatis bipinnulata
Rainbow runner

Circumtropical in distribution, adults are found both in oceanic and coastal waters where they feed on crustacean zooplankton and small fish. Their streamlined bodies are silvery to blueish with two blue stripes either side of a bright yellow stripe which all run the length of its body. Reaches a maximum total length of 180cm (commonly 90cm) and found in depths of 0–150m (commonly 2–10m).

Pseudocaranx dentex
Cavalley or guelly jack

Although this species has been recorded down to depths of 238m it is predominantly an inshore species in depths of 10–25m. It has a silver to pale blueish-green body with a pale yellow stripe and a dark spot on the edge of its operculum in line with its eye. In small groups it forages by suction feeding, filtering the sand for plankton and invertebrates which are buried. Maximum total length 122cm, commonly 40cm.

Seriola rivoliana
Almaco jack

Found in small groups this silver-coloured jack is easily distinguished by its high back and the dark diagonal line either side of its head from its lips to the front of its first dorsal fin. An inquisitive fish, it approaches divers attracted by the bubbles. They predate on fish and invertebrates and have pelagic eggs. Reaching a total maximum length of 160cm (though commonly 90cm) they are found in depths of 5–245m and are circumglobal in distribution.

Trachinotus ovatus
Pompano

A silver-coloured fish with up to five dark spots at the front of its body and black ends to its tail, dorsal and anal fins. It is common in large shoals in shallow water, often in areas with a large amount of surge, feeding on fish, molluscs and small crustaceans. Maximum total length 70cm, commonly 35cm. Historically it has been consumed by humans. Pompano are widely distributed along the African Atlantic coast and mid-Atlantic Islands. Spawning at St Helena occurs in January and February.

Uraspis helvola
Whitetongue jack
A predominately nocturnal species found over sandy habitats and at the edge of rocky reefs. This silver fish is found in depths of 50–300m and reaches a maximum total length of 58cm. Found in the South Atlantic at Ascension and St Helena and also in the Indian and Pacific Oceans.

Lutjanidae

Lutjanus jocu
Dog snapper
This subtropical fish is found in both the eastern and western Atlantic in depths of 2–40m. Juveniles of the species have been found in rivers and estuaries. They grow up to a total length of 128cm (though commonly 60cm) and predate on fish and invertebrates including crabs, shrimps, gastropods and cephalopods. Light grey to reddish-brown body with a pale triangle from bottom of eye to back edge of mouth and blue dots under eye. They have two large sharp teeth at the front of the upper jaw. Rarely sighted at St Helena it has been recorded at Torm's Ledge.

Sparidae

Diplodus sargus helenae
St Helena white seabream
Reaching up to 23cm standard length this species is endemic to St Helena. Part of the porgy or seabream family this fish has a silvery-grey body with vertical stripes, a dark patch on the base of the tail and a pointed head. Found in shallow water (relatively common 5 15m) in pairs or small groups. Juveniles are often seen over sand at night.

Mullidae

Mulloidichthys martinicus
Yellow goatfish

The yellow goatfish has a white body with yellow tail and a distinctive yellow stripe down its body. Goatfish have the ability to change their coloration dependent on what they are doing and so often can appear much darker almost red-brown in colour. It has two barbels under its chin (containing chemosensory organs) which it uses to search for prey (mainly small invertebrates) in sandy or muddy areas. Reaching around 40cm total length it is found in depths of 0–49m (usually 0–35m). Often seen in small schools, especially around the stern of the Papa Nui.

Kyphosidae

Kyphosus sectatrix
Bermuda sea chub
Found in depths down to 30m they are common in groups in the shallows (1–3m), seeming to prefer wave surged areas, for example over Long Ledge. Reaching a maximum total length of 76cm sea chub feed mainly on seaweeds but will also take small crustaceans and molluscs. They have a deep body and are grey to silver in colour with faint yellow stripes, although entirely bright yellow (xanthochromic) individuals have been seen.

Chaetodontidae

Chaetodon sanctaehelenae
St Helena butterflyfish
This species is endemic to
Ascension and St Helena living
mainly in rocky areas from
1–25m. It has a silvery-white
body with bright yellow dorsal,
anal and caudal (at base) fins and
it has a dark yellow stripe over
its eye. Reaching a maximum
length of 18cm, this species is
monogamous. Huge shoals can
be seen over wrecks and rocky
reefs. This species has also been
recorded cleaning parasites
off pipefish in surface waters.
Juveniles are often solitary hiding
in crevices and are seen during
January to March. It gets its local
name "cunningfish" from its ability
to eat the bait off the end of hooks
without getting caught.

Prognathodes dichrous
Hedgehog butterflyfish

Usually seen in pairs in depths of 15–35m over rocky or gravel substrate. Can be found in shallower waters in caves or under ledges and down to 120m. Endemic to Ascension and St Helena it reaches a maximum size of 16cm. It has distinct coloration with a chocolate brown head and lower half of body with white above. It feeds on benthic invertebrates.

Pomacanthidae

Centropyge aurantonotus
Flameback angelfish

A small bright blueish-purple fish with yellow dorsal and caudal fin. Generally found in deeper water below 20m they have also been reported from shallow water. Seen living in boulder habitats hiding in the gaps. Recorded only from Torm's Ledge, Speery Island and Egg Island in depths of 25–30m.

Cirrhitidae

Amblycirrhitus pinos
Red-spotted hawkfish

This species is relatively common on rocky reefs and amongst coralline algae from 0–25m. It has alternate brown and white stripes over its body and a dark head with numerous red spots. This hawkfish is found on the seabed under boulder or ledges or in crevices, found resting on their large pectoral rays. They predate on benthic crustaceans and small fish and grow to a maximum size of 9.5cm standard length.

Pomacentridae

Abudefduf saxatilis
Sergeant-major

Body is greyish-white with
five distinctive vertical black
bars, giving it its local name
fivefinger. During courtship and
when guarding their demersal
eggs the males are dark blue/
purple in colour. The egg patches
which adhere to the rocks are
a distinctive purple coloration.
Maximum size 23cm and
distributed in subtropical and
tropical waters of the Atlantic
in depths of 0–20m. Juveniles
are found in tide pools, with
adults found inshore on rocky
reefs where they feed on algae,
invertebrate larvae, small
crustaceans and fish.

Chromis multilineata
Brown chromis

Common in large numbers over rocky reefs they feed in the water column on plankton, in particular copepods. They have a brownish-grey or olive-brown coloured body with a black spot near the base of the pectoral fin. In this species on Ascension and other areas, but not on St Helena, they also have a white spot near the rear base of the dorsal fin. Found to 60m though common to 15m they reach a maximum total length of 20cm, commonly 12cm. They form distinct pairs during breeding and the males guard the eggs which are adhered to rocky surfaces. Large shoals of juveniles seen in January to March.

Chromis sanctaehelenae
St Helena damselfish

An endemic species to St Helena, this damselfish is dusky grey to black in coloration. It is generally larger than the St Helena Gregory reaching a total standard length of 13cm. Found on bedrock, boulder and cobble habitat usually up in the water column and often in small shoals. In depths of 5–35m.

Stegastes sanctaehelenae
St Helena Gregory

An endemic species to St Helena, this damselfish is common on the rocky reefs in inshore waters. They have a dark purple/black body with a blue tinge to the edge of its fins; juveniles have a bright blue body with white tail and dart quickly under rocks when approached. They form distinct pairs during breeding and the males aerate and guard the eggs which are adhered to rocky surfaces. They reach a total length of 11.5cm.

Labridae

Bodianus insularis
Island hogfish

Endemic to the islands of
Ascension, St Helena and St Paul's
Rocks. Juveniles are a bright
yellow whereas adults are pink/
red/purple in coloration with a
blue edge to their dorsal fin. They
are protogynous hermaphrodites
i.e. they start life as females
and later in life change sex to
become males. They display
sexual dichromatism with the
males generally being duller in
coloration than the females. Active
only during the day down to 60m
(though usually in shallower
water less than 35m), they are
carnivorous predators living on
rocky habitats. The juveniles are
cleaner fish.

Thalassoma sanctaehelenae
St Helena wrasse

An endemic species to St Helena and Ascension Island; relatively common on St Helena whereas rarely sighted on Ascension. Juveniles are pale cream/yellow with horizontal red stripes; adults have a beautiful turquoise green coloration with faint red vertical stripes. They display sexual dichromatism with the females having a paler ventral side and yellow fin margins. They grow to 21.5cm standard length and are found in rocky habitats down to 35m.

Xyrichtys blanchardi
Marmalade razorfish

This species is endemic to
Ascension Island, St Helena
(and found once on São Tomé)
and is relatively common on
sandy habitats from 5–40m. As
a defence mechanism they will
rapidly bury themselves in the
sand using the bony ridge on the
front of their heads if they feel
endangered. They grow up to
21cm standard length and are
laterally compressed. They show
great colour diversification with
small juveniles being all creamy
white and with slightly larger
juveniles being dark orangey-
brown with white vertical stripes.
Adult females are a marmalade
orange colour with five pale
vertical stripes on their body
and many fine orange stripes
on their head. Males have the
same patternation but are larger
and duller grey in colour.

Xyrichtys sanctaehelenae
Yellow razorfish

Also found on sandy habitats this species is found generally deeper than marmalade razorfish *Xyrichtys blanchardi* in depths from 17–30m. It is endemic to Ascension Island and St Helena and grows up to 23cm standard length. As a defence mechanism they will rapidly bury themselves in the sand using the bony ridge on the front of their heads if they feel endangered. Females have bright yellow coloration with a silver belly whereas the larger adult males are duller purple-grey in colour.

Scaridae

Sparisoma strigatum
Strigate parrotfish

Endemic to Ascension and St Helena this species is found over rocky habitats in depths down to 20m. Parrotfish teeth are fused together to form a "beak" which they use to scrape algae and coral off the rocks to eat, the scrape marks often visible on boulders and bedrock. They grow up to 45cm with the larger individuals being males. Two colour phases exist, the smaller, presumed females, have a yellow/grey head and front half of body with the tail being black and the larger males being dull purple/grey with black scales down their lateral line and randomly over their head. Usually seen individually or in small groups, occasional large shoals are seen in the shallows feeding on the rocks.

Tripterygiidae

Helcogramma ascensionis Ascension triplefin

Found in Lot's Wife's Ponds and at Horse Pasture Cove in the top few metres of water they are fast moving and well camouflaged against the seaweed. Olive green to brown coloured body with white spots in rows down body. They have three dorsal fins and reach a maximum size of 3.7cm standard length. Endemic to Ascension and St Helena Island.

Blenniidae

Entomacrodus textilis Textile blenny

Endemic to Ascension and St Helena the textile blenny grows up to 6cm and can be found in shallow waters (to 0.5m) in rocky areas and in tide pools, particularly where there is surf. Similar coloration to Springers blenny (light and dark green/ brown bands with square patterns) but with a blunt head. Their diet consists mainly of algae.

Ophioblennius sp.

Dark reddish-brown in coloration they can sometimes display yellow-orange to light brown bands on the head and/or body. They are found in shallow water down to 15m and feed mainly on algae but will also take zooplankton and small invertebrates. Its eggs are greenish-silver in colour and adhered to rocks. They have the local name of devilfish due to their two very sharp canine teeth.

Scartella springeri
Springers blenny

An endemic species to St Helena, Springers blenny are found in shallow reefs and tidepools, including Lot's Wife's Ponds. It reaches a size of 8cm standard length. Its eggs are demersal and are adhered to rocks. It is a pale brown to olive green in colour with many darker brown spots over its entire scaleless body and fins.

Callionymidae

Callionymus bairdi
Lancer dragonet

A small well-camouflaged fish seen darting quickly over rocks. It is sandy brown in colour with a dark and light pattern, large eyes which are on the top of a slightly flattened head and a large first dorsal fin. Found on both sandy and rocky habitats generally in shallow waters less than 10m, although occasionally deeper.

Gobiidae

Gnatholepis thompsoni
Goldspot goby

Very common on sandy/gravel bottoms from 5–32m. Well camouflaged they have a white/beige body with a darker coloured square pattern along its lower body, a dark stripe over each eye and a gold spot above the pectoral fin. They feed by sifting through the sand for organic matter or invertebrates which live there. Maximum size is 8.2cm total length. Distributed in tropical waters throughout western and eastern Atlantic and oceanic islands.

Priolepis ascensionis
Ascension goby

This small fish is found in crevices from 5–50m. It is endemic to Ascension Island and St Helena. It has alternate orange/yellow and white vertical stripes the length of its body and a black spot on its first dorsal fin. Gobies are carnivorous and feed on small invertebrates. The males act as guardians of their eggs which are laid on rocks and shells. Reaches 3.5cm total length.

Acanthuridae

Acanthurus bahianus
Ocean surgeonfish

Vary in colour from pale olive green-grey to dark brown. Very young juveniles are transparent with a silver head, later becoming pale brown with a pale blue linear pattern. Often gather in large groups in rocky habitats feeding on the seabed on algae. Surgeonfish have a sharp spine on either side of the base of the tail (caudal peduncle) which acts as a defence mechanism. Reaching a maximum total length of 38cm they are found in depths of 2–40m (commonly 2–25m). Locally this fish is called the shitty trooper.

Acanthurus coeruleus
Blue tang

(not illustrated)
Vary in colour from dark blue-purple to pale blue with the edge of both the dorsal and anal fin being bright blue. Juveniles are bright yellow in colour with blue eyes. They have a sharp spine on either side of the base of the tail (caudal peduncle) which acts as a defence mechanism. Active during the day, they feed on algae in rocky habitats from 2–40m though commonly 2–18m. Reach a maximum total length of 39cm. Only two individuals recorded on St Helena one at Speery Island and one at Long Ledge.

Scombridae

Acanthocybium solandri
Wahoo

A large silver fish with up to 30 bright blue-green vertical stripes, it reaches a total length of up to 210cm. They are fast-swimming voracious predators which feed mainly on other fish (including mackerels, scads and flyingfish) and squid. Found worldwide in tropical and subtropical oceans, this species is fished commercially, and is often caught during trolling on sportsfishing vessels. Although usually solitary it can be found in larger loose-knit groups. Within the stomach of the wahoo you can often find the trematode parasite *Hirudinella ventricosa*. IUCN Red List status of Least Concern.

Katsuwonus pelamis
Skipjack tuna

This highly migratory species forms large schools and is found in the top 260m of the ocean. It has a silver belly with 4–6 dark longitudinal bands and a darker purple-blue back. They are an opportunistic predator feeding on fish, squid, crustaceans and molluscs and even can be cannibalistic. In St Helena they spawn between September to February, with large females releasing pelagic eggs in batches, producing up to 2 million eggs in a season. They reach a maximum fork length of 110cm and can live for 8–12 years.

Thunnus alalunga
Albacore or Longfin tuna
Majority of body is silver-white with a dark blue-back and a distinctively long pectoral fin. Found worldwide in tropical and temperate waters they are a highly migratory oceanic species which feed on fish, crustaceans and squids. They inhabit the surface waters (0–250m usually 0–100m) as they prefer oxygen rich waters. Seasonal visitors to St Helena they occur when water temperatures are optimal. They have pelagic eggs. They attain a maximum fork length of 239cm and live up to 9 years. Fished commercially this species has IUCN Red List status of Near Threatened.

Thunnus albacares
Yellowfin tuna
An oceanic highly migratory species which feeds on fish, crustaceans and squids. Their back is dark blue with the body then becoming yellow then silver, with yellow fins and a sickle shaped large second dorsal fin. They have pelagic eggs and reach sexual maturity at around 90cm, attaining a maximum fork length of 140cm. Fished commercially all year round in St Helena, this species has IUCN Red List status of Near Threatened.

Thunnus obesus
Bigeye tuna
A fast-swimming, streamlined migratory species, they are found globally in tropical and temperate waters. Reaching a maximum total length of 250cm they live up to 12 years reaching maturity at four years old. Due to their ability to dive deep (down to 500m) they can feed on benthic crustaceans and also on deepwater squids. Caught by pole and line fishing in St Helena during April–June, they are locally called coffrey.

Auxis rochei bullet tuna, *Auxis thazard* frigate tuna and *Euthynnus alletteratus* little tunny are also all caught around St Helena.

Coryphaenidae

Coryphaena equiselis
Pompano dolphinfish
Found in surface waters of tropical and subtropical oceans the dolphinfish is a distinctive yellow-green colour with blue dorsal fin. A protruding forehead is a distinguishing feature of mature males. Reaching a maximum total length of 127cm they live for three to four years. A carnivorous predator they feed on squid and small fish.

Xiphiidae

Xiphias gladius
Swordfish [not illustrated]
Swordfish are a large, highly migratory, fish found in the tropical and temperate Atlantic, Pacific and Indian Oceans. They use their flat bill to stun or injure their prey, predominantly feeding on squids and a wide variety of pelagic fish including mackerel and lanternfish. Maximum recorded length is 455cm (commonly 300cm) with the females being larger than males. Sexual maturity is reached at age four and they are thought to live to at least nine years old.

Istiophoridae

Istiophorus platypterus
Atlantic sailfish [not illustrated]
A highly migratory species distributed throughout the Atlantic Ocean in depths from the surface down to 200m. Dorsally it is metallic blue in colour with a silver-white underside and distinctive bluish vertical stripes (around 20) made up of spots down each side. Unlike swordfish, the sailfish and marlin species have a rounded bill and have two keels on each side of their caudal peduncle (rather than one). Grows up to 315cm and is reported to be able to swim up to speeds of 55 kilometres per hour to hunt its prey of schooling mackerel, sardines and squid.

Kajikia albida
Atlantic white marlin [not illustrated]
This pelagic species predates on squid, flyingfish, dolphinfish, jacks and mackerel which they spear with their long bill. Also recorded as feeding on crustaceans. Distributed in the Atlantic it is reported to live to 15 years old and reaching sexual maturity between 2.5–4 years. Maximum length (upper jaw to tail fork) recorded is 290cm. IUCN Red List status of Vulnerable with the main threat being caught as bycatch in tuna longline fisheries.

Makaira nigricans
Atlantic blue marlin
This oceanic species is found in the Atlantic in depths from the surface to around 40m, although it can dive as deep as 1,000m. Thought to live to at least 20 years, reaching sexual maturity at 2–4 years and reaching a maximum total length of about 500cm. Predates on squid, mackerel, tunas and crustaceans. IUCN Red List status of Vulnerable and the population is thought to be declining.

Istiompax indica
Black marlin
(not illustrated)
A highly migratory species found in the Indian and Pacific Oceans with occasional individuals being reported in the Atlantic. Usually occur in surface waters feeding on squid, small tunas, jacks and dolphinfish. Billfish all have a high fecundity releasing up to 19 million eggs at a time. Maximum total length recorded 465cm, with a 501.7kg fish recorded as being caught at St Helena in 1963. Reaching speeds of up to 130 kilometres per hour the black marlin are one of the fastest fish. They live for up to 25 years.

Tetrapturus pfluegeri
Longbill spearfish
Found in offshore waters of the Atlantic the spearfish is similar in appearance to a marlin, however without any stripes and no bump on the head. Coloration is dark blue black dorsally with a white underneath. Diet consists mainly of squid and fish including needlefish, small tunas and jacks. Reaches a maximum fork length of 254cm.

Bothidae

Bothus mellissi
St Helena flounder

Endemic to Ascension and
St Helena in depths from
5–100m. Found on sandy
or gravel habitats it is well
camouflaged moving only when
disturbed. Similar in coloration to
Bothus lunatus peacock flounder
(found on Ascension Island)
with a sandy-coloured body and
blue-edged spots it has a smaller
pectoral fin. They are ambush
predators feeding on unsuspecting
fish and crustaceans. Maximum
total length 22cm.

Cynoglossidae

Symphurus reticulatus
Reticulate tonguefish

Found on sand and cobble habitat from 7m–45m, often completely buried in the sand. Pale yellow/brown in colour with white and darker brown mottling. Specimens seen in James Bay and at night close to the Bedgellet wreck. Endemic to St Helena.

Symphurus nigrescens
Dark tonguefish

This species is widely distributed throughout the Mediterranean and eastern Atlantic and is usually found on soft muddy clay or sandy bottoms. It has a wide diet feeding mainly on small benthic invertebrates in particular polychaetes, ophiuroids, molluscs and crustaceans. The upper surface of its body is usually dark in coloration sometimes with irregular darker blotches. Largest male specimen recorded is 11.7cm standard length. A single individual seen at night in James Bay.

Balistidae

Canthidermis sufflamen
Ocean triggerfish

This relatively large grey to brownish-grey triggerfish has a brown patch at the base of its pectoral fins. It is usually solitary or in small groups in depths of 5–60m and feeds mainly on zooplankton. Often seen in midwater it can occasionally be found hidden in large rocks crevices. Maximum total length 65cm. They create hollows in sandy areas to lay their eggs which they then guard against predation (seen spawning in February and March near Cavalley Rock, St Helena).

Melichthys niger
Black triggerfish

Coloration varies, predominately black though often has greenish, blue and yellow tinges especially around the head. It has two iridescent blue lines down the sides of its body next to the dorsal and anal fins. Circumtropical in distribution the black triggerfish is not as prolific in St Helena as in Ascension waters, with greatest numbers on the windward side of the island, however, numbers are reported to be increasing. It feeds on small fish, shrimps, and algae.

Monacanthidae

Aluterus scriptus
Scrawled filefish

A beautiful fish varying in colour from olive brown to pale grey with distinctive black spots and iridescent blue lines and dots. Found in depths of 3–120m (usually 3–20m) they have a varied diet including seaweed, hydrozoans, gorgonians, sponges, anemones and tunicates. Reach a total maximum length of 110cm and have a circumtropical distribution.

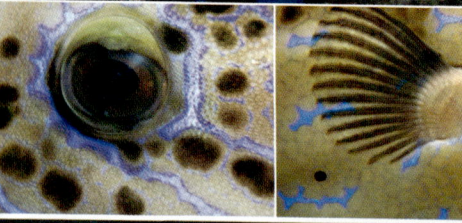

Aluterus monoceros
Unicorn filefish

A shy fish only seen occasionally, usually near drop offs, although has been seen around the wreck of the Papa Nui. Pale grey in colour with small brownish-grey spots on its upper body and a distinctive dorsal spine from which it derives its name. Distributed globally in tropical and subtropical waters it grows up to 76cm total length. Predates on benthic species.

Ostraciidae

Acanthostracion notacanthus
Island cowfish

This boxfish has a regular hexagon pattern over its blue/green body and has two sharp spines or "horns" over its eyes. Sometimes changes colour to a very pale blue. Usually found singly or in pairs over rocky, sandy or rubble habitat in depths of 3–25m. Maximum size is 50cm (total length) and it is distributed in the eastern Atlantic mainly around islands including Ascension, St Helena and São Tomé. Boxfish feed on tunicates, sponges, soft corals, small crustaceans and marine plants.

Tetraodontidae

Canthigaster sanctaehelenae St Helena sharpnose pufferfish

Endemic to St Helena and Ascension Island and found in depths from 0–45m. Pufferfish store tetrodotoxin (a strong poison) in their liver and ovaries as a defence mechanism. They are brown in colour with a light belly, numerous bright blue spots and vivid yellow eyes. Found in rocky habitats they are relatively unafraid of divers. *Canthigaster* species feed on a range of invertebrates. Maximum standard length approximately 10cm.

Sphoeroides pachygaster Blunthead puffer

Olive green-grey dorsally with a white belly and very smooth skin it reaches a total length of up to 40cm. A deepwater species occurring from 50–480m it is caught occasionally by fishermen. Using its beak-like jaw, with two extremely sharp teeth on each jaw, it predates on squid. It is found over both sandy and rocky areas and has a circumglobal distribution in both tropical and temperate waters.

Diodontidae

Chilomycterus reticulatus
Spotfin burrfish

Beige to pale olive/brown in colour except for its dark spots and occasional darker patches on its back. It is covered in large spines which lie close to its body and can inflate when threatened. Solitary creatures they are also quite territorial, often found under the same overhang or in the same small cave. They feed on molluscs, sea urchins and crustaceans. Circumsubtropical in distribution they reach a maximum size of 69.7cm

Ranzania laevis
Slender mola

This pelagic species inhabits the open ocean with a circumglobal distribution in both tropical and subtropical water in depths of 1–140m. A solitary species it predates on pelagic crustaceans. Maximum total length 100cm. A single specimen caught by fishermen at Dawson's fishing ground off St Helena.

Gempylidae

Promethichthys prometheus
Roudi escolar

This species of snake mackerel is found in deep water from 80–800m, migrating to surface waters at night to feed on fish and squid. Reaching a maximum length of 100cm (commonly 40cm) smaller individuals have been caught off Buoy's Hole at night. The larger ***Lepidocybium flavobrunneum* escolar** (pictured centre) has also been caught at St Helena on long line. This species reaches up to 200cm and is found in depths of 200–885m. Both species of escolar contain a wax ester content which if eaten in large amounts can cause keriorrhea (fish poisoning resulting in stomach cramps).

Ruvettus pretiosus
Oilfish

Locally referred to as the night barracuda, this species of snake mackerel occurs in depths of 100–800m and has been caught on longlines set at night. It has a very oily flesh, however like the other Gempylidae it contains the wax esters and so should not be consumed in great quantities.

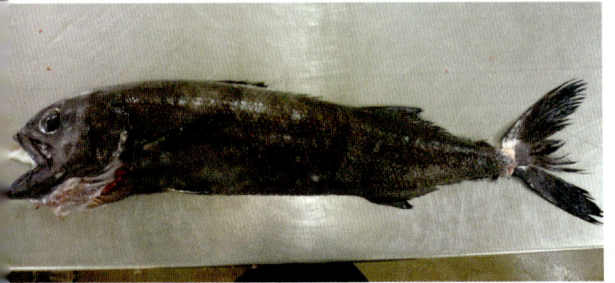

CHORDATA:
REPTILIA

CHORDATA: REPTILIA

There are over 10,000 species of reptiles in the world although most of these are terrestrial. Two species of turtle (hawksbill and green) are found in the marine environment around St Helena. There are no successful breeding beaches around St Helena, however nesting attempts on Sandy Bay beach have been recorded for green turtles. Nearby Ascension Island has the world's second largest nesting population for green turtles and the temperature of the sand on the different beaches determines the sex of the turtle hatchlings.

Hawksbill turtles *Eretmochelys imbricata* are often seen on the wreck of the Papa Nui in James Bay, St Helena

A large green turtle *Chelonia mydas* glides effortlessly through the water

Eretmochelys imbricata
Hawksbill turtle

Reaching up to 100cm in length hawksbills have a mottled brown-green shell with a jagged edge and their head has a sharp beak. This migratory species is distributed throughout the Atlantic, Pacific and Indian Oceans in tropical and subtropical areas. A long-lived species, hawksbills don't become sexually mature until they are between 20–40 years old. During a single breeding season females will lay between 3–5 clutches of eggs in nests dug on sandy beaches. Their diet varies between regions and includes predation on sponges, algae, soft corals, jellyfish and sea anemones. IUCN Red List status of Critically Endangered.

Chelonia mydas
Green turtle

Green turtles migrate for long distances between their coastal feeding areas and sandy beaches, often on isolated oceanic islands, on which they nest. Females breed every 3–4 years, laying on average 720 eggs in six clutches. Hatchlings leave the nest at night after 45–60 days making their way to the sea, heading out on ocean currents. Green turtles reach maturity at around 17–35 years and generally return to their natal nesting sites to breed. Adults are predominantly herbivorous feeding on marine plants. IUCN Red List status of Endangered.

CHORDATA: MAMMALIA

CHORDATA: MAMMALIA

Almost all mammals give birth to live young (viviparous) and have mammary glands with which their feed their young on milk. They breath air and have hairy bodies. They include both terrestrial and marine species (seals, whales, dolphins, porpoises, dugongs, etc) and this group includes the largest animal on the planet, the blue whale. Around St Helena there are three resident populations of dolphins as well as seasonal visits by migratory humpback whales. Occasional sightings of **Blainville's beaked whale** *Mesoplodon densirostris*, **sperm whale** *Physeter macrocephalus*, **pygmy sperm whale** *Kogia breviceps* and **dwarf sperm whale** *Kogia sima* have also been made around St Helena.

Rough-toothed dolphins *Steno bredanensis*, although not commonly seen, can be found around St Helena year-round

Pantropical spotted dolphins *Stenella attenuata* (left) provide amazing acrobatic displays for passing boats

Megaptera novaeangliae
Humpback whale

Humpback whales frequent St Helena's waters annually from June to December. In June individual adults are seen, with sightings of mother and a single calf being reported from July onwards. This suggests that soon after the whales arrive in St Helena waters they give birth, after an 11.5-month gestation period. They feed the calf milk that is 45–60% fat until it is strong enough to make the migration to their summer feeding grounds. They grow to up to 16m and live to around 48 years. Living off their fat reserves during winter months, humpbacks feed during the summer on krill and small shoals of fish.

Steno bredanensis
Rough-toothed dolphin

A resident species to St Helena, the rough-toothed dolphin is only seen occasionally, usually seen travelling in small numbers alongside bottlenose dolphins. It is a large dolphin (reaching up to 2.8m) with a slender nose on a conical shaped head. Body pale grey with a darker grey back and dorsal fin and in older individuals there are pinkish or white markings under the mouth. They predate on fish and squid. Named rough-toothed for the fine vertical wrinkles on its teeth.

Tursiops truncates
Bottlenose dolphin

Generally sighted all year round they are usually seen in groups of 1–38 individuals, often bow riding. They search for their fish prey using echolocation. From July to September each year a small group of bottlenose herd flyingfish into James Bay, causing the fish to take flight smashing into the wharf wall and making easy meals for the dolphins. This large grey dolphin can reach up to 4m in length and live to 40 years. Mating is belly to belly and after a gestation period of around 12 months usually only a single calf is born.

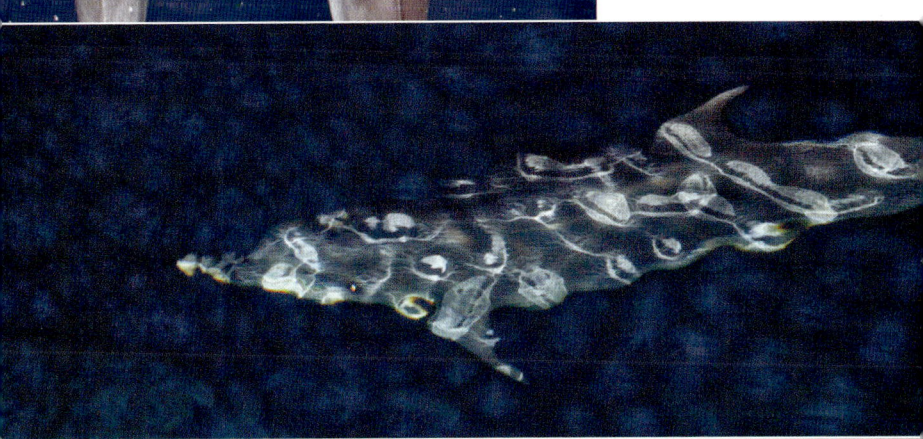

Stenella attenuata
Pantropical spotted dolphin
Locally called "porpoise" and once taken for food, the pantropical spotted dolphins are seen on the leeward side of the island all year round. Recorded in groups of 5–425 individuals (commonly around 200–300) they are a very active species often seen making huge leaps clear of the water. Smaller than the bottlenose dolphin they reach a maximum size of 2.5m. Circumglobal in distribution in tropical and subtropical waters. Feeds on fish and small squid.

CHORDATA: AVES

CHORDATA: AVES

This vertebrate group can be differentiated in that they all have feathers, a beak with no teeth and lay eggs with hard shells. There is great diversity in the species beyond that, some can fly, some can't, and some can barely walk. Some can live a very long time (albatrosses can live up to 60 years) and some travel immense distances to feed or to breeding grounds. Seabirds are defined as species which spend a large proportion of their time feeding at sea. There are nine species of breeding seabird on St Helena (with an extra species still being investigated) and there are three extinct species of seabird including the St Helena shearwater and the St Helena petrel (their demise probably caused by the introduction of mammalian predators).

Usually only visitors to St Helena, the red-footed booby *Sula sula* has recently been reported nesting within the Sandy Bay National Conservation Area.

A brown booby *Sula leucogaster* and a black noddy *Anous minutus* both nesting on Egg Island

A brown noddy *Anous stolidus* egg laid in a scrape on the ground

A fairy tern *Gygis alba* and chick on a tree in Jamestown

Oceanodroma castro
Madeiran storm petrel

The smallest of St Helena's breeding seabirds it is black with a distinctive white rump. There are two separate breeding seasons on St Helena; a "cool" breeding season from March to August and a "hot" breeding season from October to January. Nesting occurs in rock crevices on Egg Island and a single egg is laid which hatches after 40 days. Chicks fledge after around 11 weeks. Storm petrels have specially modified "tubes" atop their bills. This special organ allows them to drink salt water and then dispose of the salt. You can sometimes see drops of concentrated saline being "sneezed" out of these tubes. It feeds during the day mostly on planktonic crustaceans, fish and squid by pattering, dipping and also by surface-seizing. Anticipated taxonomic revision could result in the reclassification of this species as an endemic to Ascension and St Helena.

Phaethon aethereus
Red-billed tropicbird

The red-billed tropicbird has a white body with scattered black feathers, with adults exhibiting a long white tail and prominent red bill. Juveniles are yellow-billed and lack the long tail. A single egg is laid in a crevice in the rock on steep cliffs and is incubated for 43 days. Chicks will fly after 80 to 100 days. It feeds mostly on small fish, especially flyingfish, but will also take squid. Most prey is caught by plunge-diving but flyingfish are sometimes taken in flight. Distributed in the tropical Atlantic, eastern Pacific and Indian Oceans, the population occurring on St Helena is internationally important. The colony on Great Stone Top is the largest on St Helena.

Sula leucogaster
Brown booby

One of the least abundant seabird species around St Helena with fewer than 20 breeding pairs, mostly on Shore Island. Brown boobies are similar in shape to masked boobies, but smaller and more slender. The upper body is chocolate brown with a sharply defined white belly and a large bright yellow bill. Juveniles have pale grey bellies and greyish bills. Global population is estimated to be 200,000 individuals. The nest is a small platform of pebbles, seaweed and debris on a cliff ledge. Two eggs are laid but only one chick survives. Incubation takes around 45 days and chicks fledge after around 120 days. Its diet comprises mainly of flyingfish and squid and other small fish which are usually caught by plunge-diving, although it can also snatch prey at the water surface.

Sula dactylatra
Masked booby

Masked boobies are wide-ranging seabirds that can normally be found over pelagic waters. They make impressive dives into the sea to feed on large species of shoaling fish, especially flyingfish, and also large squid. Found on Shore and George Island, and since 2009, masked boobies have also been documented breeding on the Sandy Bay area of mainland St Helena and are now commonly seen around Lot's Wife and Blue Point. On St Helena they breed all year round, usually laying two eggs and with incubation taking around 45 days. The older chick kills the younger one (siblicide) and therefore only one chick will survive to fledging, which is 120 days after hatching. Females have a honking call while the males make a whistling sound.

Anous stolidus
Brown noddy

The brown noddy is a large chocolate-brown coloured tern with a white forehead and a pale grey crown. It is the largest of the noddies and has a global distribution in tropical and subtropical areas. On St Helena they occur on the majority of the offshore islets with Egg Island being the most important offshore breeding ground. Breeding season is November to March, and females lay a single egg which they incubate for around 35 days. The nest is a simple scrape with little or no lining. Chicks fledge around eight weeks old. Speery Island is the most important offshore islet during the non-breeding season. These birds are very good at protecting their nests and will dive bomb if you get to close.

Anous minutus
Black noddy
One of the most abundant seabirds around St Helena it is similar to the brown noddy, but smaller and its plumage is darker brown almost black with a more prominent white crown. There are approximately 1,500–2,500 breeding pairs around the coast of St Helena with Egg Island and the cliff faces opposite Egg Island hosting the largest colonies. Females lay a single egg which is incubated for around 35 days. The nest is a cream-yellow bracket formed of feathers and seaweed mixed with guano and cemented to a narrow cliff ledge. Chicks fledge after 85 to 100 days. Birds usually forage relatively close to the breeding colony and they predate on fish and squid.

Sterna fuscata
Sooty tern

A large tern which is black on its back and crown with white underneath and with a distinctive forked tail. Juveniles are dark brown, spotted with white and have a small white belly patch. Also known as a "wideawake" due to the loud calls they make. Present all year around on St Helena, Speery Island is the most important offshore islet for this species. Nesting on rocky areas in an unlined, shallow scrape or on bare rock, females lay between 1–3 speckled eggs which have a short incubation period (28–30 days) and chicks can fly at around 60 days. Sooty terns feed on small fish and squid, but also occasionally take crustaceans. The species is reliant upon prey driven to the surface by predatory fish (for example tuna), especially when breeding.

Gygis alba
Fairy tern or white tern
A small white seabird with a long thin black bill and rings of black feathers around the eyes. Juveniles are creamier in colour and have dull brown edges to the feathers of the upper-parts. Common on St Helena in Jamestown and the cliff faces from James Bay to Rupert's Bay and on Thompson Valley Island. A single egg is laid on a bare rock or tree branch with peak laying period during July. Incubation takes 36 days and chicks have well-developed feet to hold onto the tree branches. The chick fledges after seven weeks. Fairy terns predate on small fish caught by surface dipping.

ALGAE

ALGAE

Algae range in size from tiny single celled organisms found in the plankton to large multicellular seaweeds. Seaweeds use chlorophyll to photosynthesise to create food, utilising nutrients in the water including ammonia, nitrates and phosphates. There are three different divisions of seaweed the green algae (Chlorophyta), brown algae (Phaeophyta), and the red algae (Rhodophyta).

The large brown drift kelp *Ecklonia maxima* is sometimes found floating in the waters around St Helena

Turrets of the red coralline algae can be found on boulders in the shallows

The harpoon weed *Asparagopsis taxiformis* is one of the most common red algae species found in St Helena

CHLOROPHYTA

Acetabularia sp.
Green mermaid's wine glass
A single round green cap on a thin stalk which grows usually in protected rocky habitats. Found singly or in small groups. Small, usually less than 10mm.

Bryopsis plumosa
Evenly branched mossy feather weed
A dark green (sometimes with a blue tinge) seaweed with a soft feather-like appearance. Reaches 150mm tall and is found on rocky substrate.

Caulerpa racemosa
Sea grapes
This green seaweed has numerous long cylindrical branches which are anchored to the substrate with many round spheres attached. A widely distributed species in temperate and tropical seas. Reproduction can be both sexual and asexual (by fragmentation). Common in Rupert's Bay and James Bay in shallow water.

Codium spongiosum
Green cushion algae
A spongy dark green algae growing on rocky substrates in shallow, relatively unexposed areas. The thallus (or leaves) are globular with a velvety surface and rounded edges.

Codium taylorii
Dead man's fingers
Dichotomously branched, this green algae is medium to dark green in colour. It has a spongy texture with a velvet-like appearance due to a covering of fine hairs. Found in rocky habitats including in Lot's Wife's Ponds.

Ulva lactuca
Sea lettuce
A transparent light green flat leaf with irregular margins and with a single, short, disc-shaped holdfast. Found along the tide line and in rock pools with a worldwide distribution.

Valonia sp.
Elongated sea pearls
Spherical or elongated oval-shaped dark green single cell bladders or bubbles each with a glass-like sheen. Grow in clusters. Recorded from the wrecks of the Frontier, Bedgellet and Papa Nui and at Long Ledge.

PHAEOPHYTA

Dictyota dichotoma
Y-branched algae
Although it often appears green to blue-green in colour this is a species of brown algae. Common in rocky habitats they form mats over the substrate. Each branch has a distinctive fork at the end.

Padina pavonica
Peacocks tail or
white scroll algae
Greyish-white to pale brown flat leafy blades with rounded edges, they form large clusters on rocky substrates. A brown algae distributed in the Atlantic Ocean and Mediterranean Sea.

RHODOPHYTA

Asparagopsis taxiformis
Harpoon weed
A tree-like red algae with a thick stem and numerous bushy branches which are dusky pink in colour. Native to the Pacific Ocean it has been introduced to other areas. Edible with a peppery flavour, often used in tuna dishes in Hawaii. Grows on rocky habitats around St Helena, often covering extensive areas.

Liagora viscida
Slimy liagora
A soft dichotomously branched red seaweed formed of cylindrical thin filaments. It is white in colour as the thallus (branches) are calcified (made of calcium carbonate), however it has a pinkish-purple tinge. Present only during spring and summer it disappears during winter months when the thallus disintegrates. Reaches a size of 50–120mm, occurring in rocky habitats to 25m.

Wrangelia pencillata
The most abundant species of red algae found on St Helena, *Wrangelia* is found covering rocky substrates. It has a soft bushy appearance with bright red tips.

Mesophyllum brachycladum
Thin coralline crust

A dusky pink to sometimes almost purple encrusting coralline algae with a white edge. Recorded from St Helena, Canary Islands, São Tomé and Príncipe Islands.

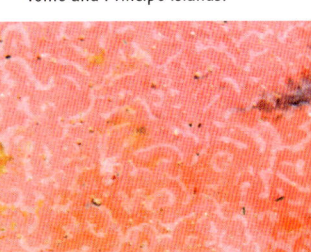

There are several species of coralline algae found encrusting the rocks in the inshore waters around St Helena, predominately in the shallows. They use lime in their composition to act as a deterrent against grazing predators. Often identification of coralline algae is difficult requiring microscopic examination. Species found on St Helena include *Neogoniolithon mamillosum* (pictured left) and *Neogoniolithon mamillare* (below left and right).

Rhodoliths and maerl

Coral-like structures made from calcium carbonate that are in fact red coralline algae can be seen at several locations around St Helena. These colourful structures called rhodoliths or maerl are unattached to the seabed and create an excellent habitat which is rich in benthic marine species. Rhodoliths produce energy through photosynthesis.

CYANOBACTERIA

Cyanophyta
Blue-green algae

Thin filamentous fuzzy masses usually dark burgundy brown to red in colour. Several different species occur, each requiring microscopic examination of filaments for identification. Often attached to other plants in well-lit areas, they obtain their energy through photosynthesis.

WRECKS

WRECKS

From historical records at least 24 shipwrecks have occurred in the waters around St Helena (both close inshore and further offshore). The older of these wrecks, almost constructed entirely of wood, are likely to have few remains left of them, being broken up by rough seas. During a very bad sea in 1846 somewhere between 12 and 27 ships were driven ashore and it is assumed any artefacts were salvaged leaving little evidence left in the sea of their presence. Eight wrecks remain in good condition to provide interesting dive sites. The Protection of Wrecks and Marine Archaeological Ordinance, enacted in 2014, protects these shipwrecks and other marine archaeological artefacts. Regulations include no wreck penetration, no sand extraction around the wrecks, no taking of any archaeological artefacts, no taking of groundfish species and no spearfishing on the wrecks. In 1987 an artificial reef made of old car bodies was established at a site off Breakneck valley. In following years, more cars, a bus and a steel and a wooden lighter were also sunk at this site with the purpose of providing additional habitat for marine species. All vehicles were cleaned of oil and engines removed prior to disposal. The site is in 25–30m of water and makes an interesting dive. The practise of creating artificial reefs on St Helena is now strictly regulated.

A shoal of glasseye snapper *Heteropriacanthus cruentatus* hide within the wreck of the Frontier

Papa Nui

The steam ship Papa Nui was built in 1898 in Plymouth and was a passenger cargo ship. Length 131m and gross tonnage of 6,372 tons. On route from the UK to Australia with 324 emigrants and all their possessions on board she caught fire on 5 September 1911. The vessel made it to St Helena and everyone was taken to safety, however the ship could not be saved and later the remaining hull was scuttled in the bay. The vessel was salvaged in the 1980s. The stern post can be seen breaking the sea surface in James Bay and on calm days the whole wreck outline can be seen from Ladder Hill. She lies in 6–12m.

Spangereid
Built in Glasgow in 1896. Originally called the Fairport she was renamed Spangereid by her Norwegian owners. Carrying a cargo of coal from Africa to Sweden she caught fire in the coal bunkers while at her moorings in James Bay and sank in 1920. She lies in 8m depth.

Darkdale

A British Royal Navy Fleet Auxiliary (8,145 ton) which was anchored in James Bay from 6 August 1941 and was sunk by a German U-boat (U−68) on the 22 October that year. This wreck is a war grave and the casualties are remembered on the Cenotaph on the wharf. She lies in 33−48m.

Witte Leeuw (White Lion)

A cargo ship sunk in action by two Portuguese carracks in 1613 in James Bay. She was carrying a cargo of spices and diamonds and a salvage operation in the 1970s recovered Chinese Ming porcelain, tons of pepper and some cannons but no diamonds. Today she lies in 33m of water and all that remains is the ballast stones, several cannons and an anchor.

Bedgellet

Brought to the island from the UK to support the team which were salvaging the Papa Nui, she was secured to the stern post during salvage operations. When salvage work was discontinued the Bedgellet was left tied to the stern post, however during a storm she broke away and caused damage to other boats in the harbour. After this incident the St Helena Government decided to sink the vessel in 2001 as an artificial reef. The site chosen was near Long Ledge in 18m for both snorkelers and scuba divers to enjoy.

Frontier

A fishing trawler (originally from the Far East), it was under surveillance from the Indian Ocean as it was suspected to be smuggling a large amount of drugs. The vessel called into St Helena for respite claiming they needed water, and the St Helena Government took this opportunity to search the vessel, including the surrounding seabed. No heroin was detected however a large amount of cannabis was found under the cooker in the galley. The vessel was confiscated and anchored in James Bay during the court case and subsequent imprisonment of the Dutch captain and crew. In 1994 the St Helena Government sunk the vessel in 27m off Lemon Valley as an artificial reef.

Portzic

Owned by a Frenchman this wooden fishing vessel turned up on St Helena after fishing further south. It fished using pole and line and other fishing methods to catch tuna mainly at the seamounts (Bonaparte and Cardno) around St Helena. Due to bad debts by the owner the vessel was repossessed by the bank. In 2008 water was coming in through the corking in the wooden planks and, as it was too old and unrepairable, it was sunk as an artificial reef next to the wreck of the Frontier in 27m off Lemon Valley.

Atlantic Rose

A German chef arrived on St Helena on a yacht and liked the island. He decided to set up a wholesale business bringing in goods from overseas and so purchased the Atlantic Rose (originally called the Bridget 2) to bring in the goods from South Africa including motorcars. He got into trouble on the island and was deported and the vessel was sold. Two local brothers purchased the boat and converted it into a fishing vessel, using it to fish mainly at Bonaparte seamount for tuna by pole and line. It was moored at an anchorage below Ladder Hill, however during bad weather it broke its moorings and an inshore wind took it onto rocks and damaged the hull at the bow. A salvage team brought the vessel to the wharf but the damage was too great to repair so it was sunk in 12m at Young's Valley. Heavy seas which followed brought the wreck into shallower water and it now lies in 8m.

Glossary

abductor muscle – muscles in bivalves used to close the shell

anterior – to the front

aperture – an opening or hole in the gastropod shell

apex – the tip or highest point of the shell

carnivorous – predatory, feeding on other animals

caudal fin – the tail fin

caudal penducle – the narrow part of the fish body where the tail attaches

class – a taxonomic category that ranks above family and below phylum

cerata – projections on the backs of nudibranchs used to increase surface area for absorption of oxygen

colonial – a community of animals or plants of one species living close together or forming a physically connected structure

circumglobal – found all around the world

detritus – waste or organic matter produced by decomposition of dead animals or plants

dichotomous – in which the branch is divided into two

dorsal – on the back

encrusting – crust like, thin

family – a taxonomic category

fecund – producing or capable of producing a large number of offspring

fork length – length from the tip of the snout to the v in the centre of the tail

genus – a taxonomic category that ranks above species and below family, a group of animal or plants which have common characteristics

herbivores – feed on plants

hinge – a joint in between the shells of a bivalve

IUCN Red List – International Union for Conservation of Nature list which assesses the conservation status of species

lateral – on the side

mantle – soft, exterior membrane of the body of a mollusc, usually in the form of flaps, and enclosing the mantle cavity which protects the gills

mottling – blotches of different colours or shades

operculum – a structure which covers an aperture including a gill cover on fish or a hard plate used by molluscs to cover the shell opening when they have retreated inside

phylum – a taxonomic category that ranks below kingdom and above class

posterior – towards the back

rhinophore – sensory organs (taste and smell) found on the head of nudibranchs to help detect food and mates. Often club shaped, they are retractable

ribs – raised folds on the surface of a shell

sesslle – immobile, fixed in one place

siphon – a tubular organ in an aquatic animal through which water is drawn in or expelled

species – a group of living organisms consisting of individuals which are similar and are able to exchange genes or can interbreed. The species is the principal natural taxonomic unit and ranks below genus

standard length – length from the tip of the snout to the end of the last vertebrae

substrate – surface on which an animal or plant lives, such as rock or seaweed

total length – length from the tip of the snout to the end of the compressed tail

ventral – on the bottom side or belly

vesicles – fluid or air filled sac or cavity

whorl – each turn of a spiral on a shell

xanthochromic – unusually yellow pigmentation in an animal often associated with the lack of red pigmentation and its replacement with yellow. The cause is usually genetic but may also be diet.

References

Amaoka, K. and Imamura, H. 2000. A new flounder, *Monolene helenesis* (Pleuronectiformes: Bothidae) from the eastern tropical Atlantic. *Ichthyological Research* 113: 1–5.

Branch, G.M., Griffiths, C.L., Branch, M.L. and Beckley, L.E. 2010. *Two Oceans, a guide to the marine life of southern Africa.*

Brook, G. 1889. Report on the Antipatharia. In Challenger report, Zoology.

Cadenat, J. and Marchal, E. 1963. Résultats des campagnes oceanographiques de la Reine-Pokou aux iles Sainte-Helene et Ascencion. *Bulletin de l'Institut Francais d'Afrique Noire* 4: 1235–1368.

Carlgren, O. 1941. Papers from Dr Th. Mortensen's Pacific Expedition 1914–16. LXX. The Actiniaria and Zoantharia of St Helena.

Chace, F.A.J. 1966. Decapod crustaceans from St Helena Island, South Atlantic. Proceedings of The United States National Museum 118: 623–662. BioStor. Available from http://biostor.org/reference/85473 [accessed 18 December 2012].

Chace, F.A.J. 1968. A new crab of the genus *Cycloes* (Crustacea; Brachyura; Calappidae) from St Helena, South Atlantic Ocean. *Proceedings of the Biological Society of Washington* 81: 605–612.

Choat, J.H. 2006. An ecological survey of the St Helena and Ascension Island populations of the jack (*Epinephelus adscensionis*) with a review of management options.

Cunningham, J.T. and Kirkpatrick, R. 1910. On the marine fishes and invertebrates of St Helena By J.T. Cunningham M.A.,F.Z.S. With description of new species of Hydrozoa and Porifera, by R. Kirkpatrick, F.Z.S. *Proc. Zool. Soc. Lond.* 9.

Day, J.H. 1949. On the Polychaeta collected by Mr J Colman at St Helena. Journal of the Linnean Society of London, *Zoology* 41: 434–451.

Debelius, H. 2001. *Crustacea guide of the world.*

Debelius, H. and Kuiter, R.H. 2007. *Nudibranchs of the world.*

Edwards, A.J. 1993. New records of fishes from the Bonaparte Seamount and Saint Helena Island, South Atlantic. *Journal of Natural History* 27: 493–503.

Edwards, A.J. and Glass, C.W. 1987a. The fishes of Saint Helena Island, South Atlantic Ocean. I. The shore fishes. *Journal of Natural History* 21: 617–686.

Edwards, A.J. and Glass, C.W. 1987b. The fishes of Saint Helena Island, South Atlantic Ocean. II. The pelagic fishes. *Journal of Natural History* 21: 1367–1394. doi: 10.1080/00222938700770871.

Eschmeyer, W.N. 1971. Two new Atlantic scorpionfishes. Proceedings of the California Academy of Science 37: 501–507. Available from http://onlinelibrary.wiley.com/doi/10.1002/cbdv.200490137/abstract [accessed 13 December 2012].

Fricke, R. 1982. A new species of the genus *Callionymus* from St Helena (Teleostei: Callionymidae). Annali del museo civico di storia naturale Giacomo Doria 84: 393–399.

Gislen, T. 1933. Papers from Dr Th. Mortensen's Pacific Expedition 1914–16. LXVII. A small collection of crinoids from St Helena.

Gomon, M.F. and Lubbock, R. 1980. A new hogfish of the genus *Bodianus* (Teleostei: Labridae) from islands of the Mid-Atlantic. *Northeast Gulf Science* 3: 104–111.

Grave, S. De. 2007. On the occurrence of *Gnathophylleptum tellei* D'Udekem D'Aoz 2001 (Decapoda, Gnathophyllidae) in St Helena, South Atlantic Ocean. *Crustaceana* 80: 893–895.

Gunther, A. 1869. Report on a second collection of fishes made at St Helena by J.C.Melliss, Esq. *Proceedings of The Zoological Society of London:* 238–239.

Hartog, J.C. Den and Tiirkay, M. 1991. *Platypodiella georgei* spec. nov. (Brachyura: Xanthidae), a new crab from the island of St Helena, South Atlantic Ocean, with notes on the genus Platypodiella Guinot, 1967. *Zoologische Mededelingen* 65: 209–220.

Holthuis, L.B. 1993. *Scyllarides obtusus* spec, nov., the scyllarid lobster of Saint Helena, Central South Atlantic (Crustacea: Decapoda Reptantia: Scyllaridae). *Zoologische Mededelingen* 67: 505–515.

Humann, P. 1992. *Reef Creature Identification, Florida, Caribbean, Bahamas.*

Humann, P. 1993. *Reef Coral Identification, Florida, Caribbean, Bahamas.*

Humann, P. and Deloach, N. 1989. *Reef Fish Identification, Florida, Caribbean, Bahamas.*

Jeffreys, J.G. 1872. The Mollusca of St Helena. *The Annals and magazine of natural history; zoology, botany, and geology* 9: 262–264.

John, D.M., Prud'homme van Reime, W.F., Lawson, G., Kostermans, T.B. and Price, J.H. 2004. A taxonomic and geographical catelogue of the seaweeds of the western coast of Africa and adjacent islands. *Beihefte zur Nova Hedwigia* 127: 1–140.

Kropp, R.K. and Manning, R. 1987. The Atlantic gall crabs, family Cryptochiridae (Crustacea: Decapoda: Brachyura). *Smithsonian Contributions to Zoology*: 1–21. doi: 10.5479/si.00810282.462.

Lawson, G., John, D.M. and Price, J.H. 1993. The Marine Algal Flora of St Helena: its Distribution and Biogeographical Affinities. *Courier Forsch. Inst. Senckenberg* 159: 103–107.

MacLeod, C.D. and Bennett, E. 2007. Pan-tropical spotted dolphins (*Stenella attenuata*) and other cetaceans around St Helena in the tropical south-eastern Atlantic. *Journal of the Marine Biological Association of the United Kingdom* 87: 339–344. doi: 10.1017/S0025315407052502.

Marcus, E. 1938. Papers from Dr Th. Mortensen's Pacific Expedition 1914–16. LXIX. Bryozoenvon St Helena. *Vidensk* 101: 183–252.

Mortensen, T. 1933. Papers from Dr Th. Mortensen's Pacific Expedition 1914–16. LVI. The Echinoderms of St Helena (other than crinoids).

Moura, R.L. and Castro, R.M.C. 2002. Revision of the Atlantic sharpnose pufferfishes (Tetraodontiformes: Tetraodontidae: Canthigaster), with description of three new species. *Proceedings of the Biological Society of Washington* 115: 32–50.

Munroe, T.A. 1990. Eastern Atlantic tonguefishes (Symphurus: Cynoglossidae, Pleuronectiformes), with descriptions of two new species. *Bulletin of Marine Science* 47: 464–515.

Pawson, D.L. 1978. The echinoderm fauna of Ascension Island, South Atlantic Ocean. *Smithsonian Contributions to the Marine Sciences*: 1–31. doi: 10.5479/si.01960768.2.1.

Reid, D.G. 2011. The genus echinolittorina Habe, 1956 (Gastropoda: Littorinidae) in the eastern Atlantic Ocean and Mediterranean Sea. *Zootaxa* 2974: 1–65.

Ritchie, J. 1906. The hydroids of the Scottish National Antarctic Expedition. *Transactions of the Royal Society of Edinburgh* 45: 519–545.

Ritchie, J. 1909. Supplementary reports on the hydroids of the Scottish National Antarctic Expedition. *Transactions of the Royal Society of Edinburgh* 47: 55–101.

Rosewater, J. 1975. An annotated list of the marine mollusks of Ascension Island, South Atlantic Ocean. *Smithsonian Contributions to Zoology*: 1–41. doi: 10.5479/si.00810282.189.

Smith, E.A. 1890a. Report on the Marine Molluscan Fauna of the Island of St Helena. *Proc. Zool. Soc. Lond.*: 247–317. Available from http://biostor.org/reference/99510.

Smith, E.A. 1890b. Further additions to the known marine molluscan fauna of St Helena. *The Annals and magazine of natural history; zoology, botany, and geology* 10: 247–317.

Smith, J.L.B. 1965. *Acanthurus bahianus* Castelnau, 1855, in the Southeast Atlantic Ocean. *Copeia* 1: 110–111.

Trunov, I.A. 2006. Ichthyofauna of seamounts around the island of Ascension and St Helena Island (Atlantic ocean). *Journal of Ichthyology* 46: 493–499. doi: 10.1134/S0032945206070010.

Vaske Junior, T., Lopes de Lima, K., Ribeiro, A.C.B. and Lessa, R.P. 2008. Record of the St Helena deepwater scorpionfish, *Pontinus nigropunctatus* (Günther) (Scorpaeniformes: Scorpaenidae), in the Saint Peter and Saint Paul Archipelago, Brazil. *Pan-American Journal of Aquatic Sciences* 3: 46–48.

Werner, T.B. 1997. Recent Zooxanthellate Corals (Order: Scleractina) from Ascension and St Helena Islands, South Atlantic, with a summary of their geographic distribution in the Atlantic Ocean.

Wirtz, P. and Debelius, H. 2003. *Mediterranean and Atlantic invertebrate guide.*

Zibrowius, H. 1974. Redescription of *Sclerhelia hirtella* from Saint Helena, South Atlantic, and remarks on Indo-Pacific species erroneously referred to the same genus (Scleractinia). *Journal of Natural History* 8: 563–575. doi: 10.1080/00222937400770481.

Index

Aaptos **sp.** 11
Abudefduf saxatilis 149
Acanthocybium solandri 163
Acanthonyx sanctaehelenae 48
Acanthostracion notacanthus 171
Acanthurus bahianus 162
Acanthurus coeruleus 162
Acar domingensis 92
Acetabularia sp. 197
Acotylea sp. 34, 36
Aglaophenia parvula 28
Aglaophenia cf. *picardi* 28
Aiptasia insignis 19
albacore 164
Albunea carabus 62
algae, blue-green 202
algae, green cushion 198
algae, white scroll 199
algae, Y-branched 199
Alima neptuni 63
Alopias superciliosus 117
Alpheus cedrici 59
Alpheus paracrinitus 59
Aluterus monoceros 170
Aluterus scriptus 170
Amblycirrhitus pinos 148
Americardia media 94
Amphoriscidae 14
anemone, banded tube 19
anemone, burrowing 21
anemone, club-tipped 18, 57, 60
anemone, common sea 17
anemone, false plum 17
anemone, Forskal's sea 18
anemone, striped 20
anemone, trumpet 19
angelfish, flameback 148
Anous minutus 186, 192
Anous stolidus 186, 191
Antennarius nummifer 127
Antennarius striatus 127
Anthothoe affinis 20
Antipathozoanthus sp. 20, 26
Aplysia fasciata 87
Aplysia parvula 87
Aplysilla sp. 6
Aplysina sp. 6
Apogon axillaris 135
Arca bouvieri 92
Ariosoma mellissi 124
Ascidia sp. 111

Asparagopsis taxiformis 87, 196, 200
Astropecten sanctaehelenae 103
Astropecten variegatus 103
Aulostomus strigosus 129
Auxis rochei 164
Auxis thazard 164

Balanophyllia helenae 16, 23
Balanus trigonus 64
barnacle, common goose 64, 85
barnacle, giant barnacle 63
barnacle, pyramid barnacle 64
Berthellina cf. *edwardsi* 88
Bispira sp. 38, 42
bivalve, heart-shaped 94
blenny, Springers 159
blenny, textile 158
Bodianus insularis 153
booby, brown 186, 189
booby, masked 190
booby, red-footed 186
Bornella sp. 84
Bothus mellissi 167
Bractechlamys corallinoides 93
Brachycarpus biunguiculatus 58
Brissus unicolor 108
brittlestar, common 105
Bryopsis plumosa 197
bryozoan, cactus-bush 67
bryozoan, single horn 66, 68
Bugula cf. *dentata* 2, 67, 83
Bulbaeolidia sp. 85
bullseye, longfinned 134
burrfish, spotfin 173
Bursa corrugata pustulosa 76
butterflyfish, hedgehog 147
butterflyfish, St Helena 1, 120, 146

Cacospongia sp. 8
Calappa sp. 47
Calcinus tubularis 55
Callionymus bairdi 160
Canthidermis sufflamen 169
Canthigaster sanctaehelenae 172
Caranx crysos 137
Caranx lugubris 137

Caranx ruber 137
Carcharhinus galapagensis 117
Carcharhinus longimanus 117
cardinalfish, axillary-spot 135
Carijoa riisei 25
Caulerpa racemosa 197
cavalley 140
Centropyge aurantonotus 148
Chaetaster longipes 98
Chaetodon sanctaehelenae 1, 120, 146
Chaetopterus variopedatus 42
Charonia variegata 72
Cheilopogon nigricans 127
Cheilopogon pinnatibarbatus 127
Chelonia mydas 176, 178
Chilomycterus reticulatus 173
Chondrosia cf. *plebeja* 8
Chromis multilineata 150
Chromis sanctaehelenae 120, 151
chromis, brown 150
Cinetorhynchus rigens 58
clam, ark 92
clam, file 92
clam, white miniature ark 92
cockle, Atlantic strawberry 94
Codium spongiosum 198
Codium taylorii 198
comber, St Helena 133
Conchoderma virgatum 64
conger, Melliss's 124
Conus jourdani 79
Cookeolus japonicus 134
coral, black fan 16, 20, 26, 80, 91
coral, orange cup 16, 23
coral, snowflake 25
coral, star 24
coral, St Helena tree 25
coral, wire 26
coralline crust, thin 201
Coralliophila patruelis 74
cornetfish, Atlantic 129
Coryphaena equiselis 165
Coscinasterias tenuispina 57, 102
cowfish, island 171
cowrie, fallow 79
cowrie, St Helena 79
cowshark, sevengill 117

crab, Ascension sally lightfoot 45
crab, blood red 51
crab, decorator 48
crab, delicate swimming 50
crab, insular shore 50
crab, lesser spotted shame-faced
    47
crab, mole 62
crab, nimble spray 46
crab, sponge 8, 44, 51
crab, St Helena decorator 48
crab, tidal spray 44, 46
crab, urchin 46
Cryptosoma cristatum 47
cushion star, variable 103
Cyanophyta 202
Cymbula safiana 71
Cyphoma eludens 80
Cyphoma sp. 80
*Cypraecassis testiculus
    senegalica* 75

damselfish, St Helena 120, 151
Dardanus imperator 20, 55
dead man's fingers 198
Decapterus punctatus 138
Decapterus macarellus 138
Decapterus muroadsi 139
Decapterus tabl 139
Dendrodoris cf. *angolensis* 83
Desmanthus sp. 10
Diadema ascensionis 46, 58,
    98, 107
Dictyoceratida 5
Dictyota dichotoma 199
Didemnum sp. 113
Diodora gibberula 71
Diplodus sargus helenae 143
Dolabrifera dolabritera 86
dolphin, bottlenose 183
dolphin, pantropical spotted 180,
    183
dolphin, rough-toothed 180, 182
dolphinfish, pompano 165
dorid 83
Doriopsilla sp. 84
Doris cf. *ocelligera* 85
dragonet, lancer 160
Drillia sinuosa 74
Dromia erythropus 51
Dromia marmorea 51
Dromia personata 51
Dromia sp. 8, 44, 51
Dysidea sp. 7, 8

Echeneis naucrates 136
Echinocardium connectens 108
Echinolittorina helenae 72
Echinolittorina punctata 72
Echinometra lucunter 107
Echinoneus cyclostomus 108
echiuran, green rock 41
Ecklonia maxima 196
Ectopleura cf. *mayeri* 32
eel, ornate snake 124
Elagatis bipinnulata 140
Enchelycore anatina 121
Enchelycore carychroa 122
Enchiridium cf. *periommatum*
    35
Enoplometopus antillensis 52
Entomacrodus textilis 158
Epinephelus adscensionis 132
Eretmochelys imbricata 176,
    177
*Erosaria acicularis
    sanctahelenae* 79
Escharoides sp. 67
escolar 174
escolar, Roudi 174
Euapta lappa 100
Eucidaris tribuloides 78, 106
Eudendrium carneum 31
Eudendrium ramosum 31
eulimid, Atlantic 78
Euryozius sanguineus 51
Euryspongia sp. 5
Eurythoe complanata 39
Euthynnus alletteratus 164
Euvola turtoni 93
Exocoetus obtusirostris 127
Exocoetus volitans 127

Favia gravida 24
feather weed, evenly-branched
    mossy 197
Felimare sp. 83
Felimida cf. *atlantica* 82
Felimida cf. *clenchi* 82
filefish, scrawled 170
filefish, unicorn 170
Fiona pinnata 85
fireworm, bearded 39
flounder, St Helena 167
flyingfish 127
flyingfish, African 127
flyingfish, Bennett's 127
flyingfish, blacksail 127
flyingfish, mirrorwing 127

flyingfish, oceanic two-wing 127
flyingfish, tropical two-wing 127
frogfish 127

Gnatholepis thompsoni 161
Gnathophylleptum tellei 57
Gnathophyllum americanum 57
goatfish, yellow 144
goby, Ascension 161
goby, goldspot 161
Gorgonia 25
gorgonian, rose lace 25
Grantia (?) sp. 12
Graspus adscensionis 45
Gregory, St Helena 152
Gygis alba 186, 194
Gymnothorax miliaris 122
Gymnothorax moringa 123
Gymnothorax unicolor 123
Gymnothorax vicinus 122

Haminoea orbignyana 89
hammerhead 117
harpoon weed 87, 196, 200
hawkfish, red-spotted 148
Helcogramma ascensionis 158
hermit crab, anemone 55
hermit crab, hairy 55
hermit crab, stripy-legged 55
Hermodice carunculata 39
Hesione pantherina 40
Heteropriacanthus cruentatus
    134, 204
Hippocampus sp. 130
Hipponix grayanus 71
Hirundichthys speculiger 127
hogfish, island 153
Holanthias fronticinctus 133
Holocentrus adscensionis 128
*Holothuria (Platyperona)
    sanctori* 78, 99
*Holothuria (Thymiosycia)
    arenicola* 99
hydroid, Christmas tree 30
hydroid, red stick 31
hydroid, smoky feather 27
hydroid, solitary sponge 32
hydroid, unbranched 29
Hymedesmiidae 12
Hymeniacidon sp. 10

Ircina sp. 7
Isarachnanthus maderensis 19
Isaurus sp. 22

Istiompax indica 166
Istiophorus platypterus 165
Isurus oxyrinchus 117

jack, almaco 141
jack, bar 137
jack, black 137
jack, guelly 140
jack, whitetongue 142
Janicea antiguensis 60
Janthina exigua 77

Kajikia albida 165
Kaloplocamus ramosus 84
Katsuwonus pelamis 163
kelp, brown drift 196
Kogia breviceps 180
Kogia sima 180
Kyphosus sectatrix 145

Laleonectes vocans 50
Lepas anatifera 64, 85
Lepidocybium flavobrunneum 174
Leucandra sp. 14
Liagora viscida 200
liagora, slimy 200
Limaria hians 92
limpet, humped keyhole 71
limpet, safian 71
lizardfish, bluntnose 126
lizardfish, diamond 125
lobster, brown spiny 53
lobster, red Atlantic reef 52
lobster, red slipper 54
Lopha cristagalli 91
Luidia sagamina 104
Luria lurida oceanica 79
Lutjanus jocu 142
Lygdamis wirtzi 38, 40
Lysmata grabhami 56
Lysmata sp. 57

mackerel, yellowtail 139
Macrorhynchia filamentosa 27
Macrorhynchia philippina 27
Madracis sp. 24
Maerl 202
Makaira nigricans 166
mako, shortfin 117
Margaretta cf. *levinseni* 67
marlin, Atlantic blue 166
marlin, Atlantic white 165
marlin, black 166

marlinsucker 136
Megabalanus azoricus 63
Megaptera novaeangliae 181
Melanella atlantica 78
Melichthys niger 169
Membraniporid 68
mermaid's wine glass, green 197
Mesophyllum brachycladum 201
Mesoplodon densirostris 180
Metadromia wilsoni 51
Metapenaeopsis gerardoi 51
Metaxia rugulosa 78
metaxia, rugged 78
Microcassiope minor 49
Micromelo undatus 89
Mitrella ocellata 75
Mobula tarapacana 116, 118
mola, slender 173
Monoplex pilearis 75
moray, brown 123
moray, Caribbean chestnut 122
moray, fangtooth 121
moray, goldentail 122
moray, purplemouth 122
moray, spotted 123
moray, whitespot 121
Moreiradromia antillensis 51
Morula (Morula) consanguinea 73
moss animal, dentate 67
Mulloidichthys martinicus 144
Muraena pavonina 121
Mycale (Mycale) **sp.** 11
Myripristis jacobus 129

Nassarius sanctaehelenae 70, 73
needlefish, Ascension keeled 128
Neogoniolithon mamillare 201
Neogoniolithon mamillosum 201
noddy, black 186, 192
noddy, brown 186, 191
Notocochlis dillwynii 77
Notorynchus cepedianus 117
nudibranch, green and black 2, 67, 83
nudibranch, lynx 82
nudibranch, painter 84
nudibranch, white-patched 84

Oceanodroma castro 187
Ochetostoma baronii 41

Octopus macropus 70, 96
Octopus occidentalis 95
octopus, blanket 96
octopus, common 95
octopus, white-spotted 70, 96
oilfish 174
Ophichthus regius 124
Ophidiaster ophidianus 57, 102
Ophioblennius **sp.** 159
Ophiothrix roseocaerulans 105
ovulid, elusive 80
oyster, cockscomb 91
oyster, rock 91
oyster, wing 91

Pachycerianthus **sp.** 21
Pachygraspus loverigei 49
Padina pavonica 199
Palythoa caribbaeorum 16,21
Palythoa **sp.** 22
Panulirus echinatus 53
Paractea rufopunctata africana 49
parrotfish, strigate 157
Parvulastra exigua 103
peacock's tail 199
Pecten **sp.** 93
Pennaria disticha 30
Percnon gibbesi 46
Pericelis cf. *cata* 34, 36
periwinkle, St Helena 72
Phaethon aethereus 188
Phascolosoma (Phascolosoma) stephensoni 41
Phidiana lynceus 82
Phymactis sanctaehelenae 17
Physalia physalis 32, 77, 85, 96
Physeter macrocephalus 180
Pinna rugosa 61, 70, 90
Pisa sanctaehelenae 48
Plagusia depressa 44, 46
Platybelone argalus trachura 128
Pleurobranchus cf. *areolatus* 88
Plumapathes pennacea 16, 20, 26, 80, 91
Polinices lacteus 76
Polycarpa sp. (gr. *P. spongialis*) 111
Polycitoridae sp. 114
Polyclinum costellatum 110, 114
Polycyathus atlanticus 23

Polysyncraton sp. 113
pompano 141
Pontinus nigropunctatus 130
Pontonia cf. *pinnophylax* 61, 90
Portuguese man-of-war 32, 77, 96
Portunus anceps 50
Priolepis ascensionis 161
Prionace glauca 116, 117
Prognathodes dichrous 147
Promethichthys prometheus 174
Protopalythoa canariense 22
Pseudactinia varia 17
Pseudobiceros cf. *pardalis* 36
Pseudoboletia atlantica 106
Pseudocaranx dentex 140
Pseudocarcharias kamoharai 117
Pseudoceros sp. 35
Pseudochama cristella 91
Pseudocyphoma aureocinctum 80
Pseudosquilla ciliata 63
Pseudosquillisma oculata 63
Pteria hirundo 91
puffer, blunthead 172
pufferfish, St Helena sharpnose 172
purple sail 32, 77
Pyramidella dolabrata 78

Ranzania laevis 173
ray, Chilean devil 116, 118
razorfish, marmalade 155, 156
razorfish, yellow 156
Remora albescens 136
Remora osteochir 136
Remora remora 136
Rhincodon typus 117
Rhodoliths 202
rock hind 132
runner, blue 137
runner, rainbow 140
Ruvettus pretiosus 174
Rypticus saponaceus 133

sailfish, Atlantic 165
sand star 104
sand star, dark red 104
Sarcotragus sp. 6
scad, mackerel 138
scad, redtail 139
scad, roughear 139
scad, round 138

scad, stonebrass 139
scallop, Atlantic 93
scallop, coral 93
Scartella springeri 159
Schizoporella cf. *unicornis* 66, 68
Sclerhelia hirtella 25
Scorpaena mellissii 131
Scorpaena plumieri 131
Scorpaenodes insularis 132
scorpaenodes, Ascension 132
scorpionfish, Melliss's 131
scorpionfish, spotted 131
scorpionfish, St Helena deepwater 130
Scyllarides obtusus 54
seabream, St Helena white 143
sea chub, Bermuda 145
sea cucumber, red 78, 99
sea cucumber, sand 99
sea cucumber, yellow-banded 100
sea fern 28
sea fern, golden 27
sea goddess, harlequin blue 82
sea grapes 197
sea hare 86
sea hare, black 87
sea hare, dotted 87
seahorse 130
sea lettuce 198
sea lily, black and white 101
sea mat, Canarian 22
sea nettle 30
sea pearls, elongated 199
seaperch, St Helena 133
sea slug, orange volcano sponge 86
sea star, purple 102
sea star, St Helena 103
sea star, variegated 103
sea umbrella, warty 89
Semele modesta 94
sergeant-major 149
Seriola rivoliana 141
Serranus sanctaehelenae 133
Sertularia marginata 29
Sertularia turbinata 29
shark, blue 116, 117
shark, crocodile 117
shark, Galapagos 117
shark, oceanic whitetip 117
shark, whale 117
sharksucker 136
sharksucker, live 136

shell, Atlantic triton trumpet 72
shell, bubble 89
shell, gaudy frog 76
shell, hoof 71
shell, milk moon 76
shell, miniature melo bubble 89
shell, rude pen 61, 70, 90
shell, Senegal helmet 75
shell, white-spotted dove 75
shell, worm 81
shell, zigzag moon 77
shipworm 81
shrimp, anemone 60
shrimp, Atlantic dancing 58
shrimp, banded coral 56
shrimp, brown-striped 58
shrimp, cave 60
shrimp, fan mussel 61, 90
shrimp, mantis 63
shrimp, scarlet-striped cleaning 56
shrimp, smoothclaw snapping 59
shrimp, snapping 59
shrimp, striped bumblebee 57
shrimp, Telle's bumblebee 57
shrimp, two claw 58
shrimp, velvet 60
shrimp, white-striped cleaning 56
slug, peach side-gilled 88
slug, warty side-gilled 88
snail, common purple 77
snail, coral 74
snail, rustic rock 74
snail, St Helena mud 70, 73
snakefish 126
snapper, dog 142
snapper, glasseye 134, 204
soapfish, greater 133
soldierfish, blackbar 129
Sparisoma strigatum 157
spearfish, longbill 166
Sphoeroides pachygaster 172
Sphyrna sp. 117
sponge, hairy tube 14
sponge, orange volcano 12, 86
squirrelfish 128
starfish, eight-armed 102
starfish, long-armed 98
Stegastes sanctaehelenae 152
Stelleta sp. 10
Stenella attenuata 180, 184
Steno bredanensis 180, 182
Stenopus hispidus 56
Sterna fuscata 193
Stichopathes filiformis 26

storm petrel, Madeiran 187
Stramonita rustica 74
Styellidae sp. 111
suckerfish, white 136
Sula dactylatra 190
Sula leucogaster 186, 189
Sula sula 186
surgeonfish, ocean 162
swordfish 165
Symphurus nigrescens 168
Symphurus reticulatus 168
Symplegma brakenhielmi 112
Symplegma rubra 110, 112
Symplegma cf. *viride* 112
Synodus synodus 125

Tambja **sp.** 2, 67, 83
tang, blue 162
Tedania (*Tedania*) **sp.** 11, 12, 86
Tellina mexicana 94
Telmatactis cricoides 18, 60
Telmatactis forskalii 18
Telmatactis solidago 18
Teredo **sp.** 81
tern, fairy 186, 194
tern, sooty 193
tern, white 194
Tethyaster magnificus 104
Tetrapturus pfluegeri 166
Thalassoma sanctaehelenae
    154
Thor cf. *manningi* 18, 60
thresher, bigeye 117
Thunnus alalunga 164
Thunnus albacares 164
Thunnus obesus 164

tonguefish, dark 168
tonguefish, reticulate 168
Trachinocephalus myops 126
Trachinotus ovatus 141
Trachycaris restricta 61
Trapania **sp.** 86
Tremoctopus violacea 96
triggerfish, black 169
triggerfish, ocean 169
triplefin, Ascension 158
triton, Atlantic hairy 75
tropicbird, red-billed 188
Tropiometra carinata 101
trumpetfish 129
tuna, bigeye 164
tuna, bullet 164
tuna, frigate 164
tuna, longfin 164
tuna, skipjack 163
tuna, yellowfin 164
tunicate, encrusting social 112
tunny, little 164
Tursiops truncates 183
turtle, green 176, 178
turtle, hawksbill 176, 177

Ulva lactuca 198
Umbraculum umbraculum 89
Uraspis helvola 142
urchin, black longspined 46, 98,
    107
urchin, grey heart 108
urchin, hairy pincushion 106
urchin, little burrowing 108
urchin, rock boring 107
urchin, slate pencil 78, 106

urchin, St Helena burrowing 108
Ute (?) **sp.** 13
Ute **sp.** 13

Valonia **sp.** 199
Velella velella 32, 77, 85
Vermetid **sp.** 81
Verongula **sp.** 9

wahoo 163
whale, Blainville's beaked 180
whale, dwarf sperm 180
whale, humpback 181
whale, pygmy sperm 180
whale, sperm 180
Williamstimpsonia denticulatus
    50
worm, devil 38, 40
worm, feather duster 38, 42
worm, leopard 40
worm, parchment 42
worm, peanut 41
Wrangelia pencillata 200
wrasse, St Helena 154

Xiphias gladius 165
Xyrichtys blanchardi 155, 156
Xyrichtys sanctaehelenae 156

zoanthid, golden encrusting 20, 26
zoanthid, lumpy finger 22
zoanthid, white encrusting 16, 21
zoanthid, yellow 22
Zoanthid sp. 22
Zyzzyzus **sp.** 32